A Helping Hand
(A guide for learners)

W J Jones

First impression—September 1996

ISBN 1 85902 393 2

Printed by Gomer Press, Llandysul, Ceredigion.

To Rhian
for many a helping hand

Contents

List of illustrations

Foreword

The idea for the 'Help Llaw' articles that are printed in this book originated with Mr John Cosslett, as Executive Editor of *The Western Mail*.

He wished each one to be relatively short and to follow a simple format—an introductory point of interest followed by a discussion on some aspect of language that could be useful to those learning Welsh as a second language, supplementing in a simple way what they might have learnt in classes or during their own studies.

Many who wrote offering suggestions said that they found it useful to compile the articles in a scrapbook; then Dr Dyfed Elis-Gruffydd of Gwasg Gomer expressed an interest in publishing a selection in book form.

I wish to thank *The Western Mail* for permitting the reprinting of all the articles, and for allowing me to reproduce a number of photographs taken by its own staff photographers. In addition, I wish to thank the National Eisteddfod of Wales for allowing me to reproduce the illustration on page 47. The illustrations on pages 39, 79 (inset), 93, 133 and 141 are from personal prints.

My thanks are due also to Mr Cosslett who has done much to secure the appearance of a variety of Welsh articles in the pages of *The Western Mail* and for his 'help llaw' to me at all times. I would like also to thank those who have written to me from time to time, not least the correspondent who wrote: 'I wish I could get money for writing a column of scribbles once a week'.

Hen Bau fy Nhadau

The above heading is the adjusted title of 'Land of my Fathers', our national anthem. The words were composed by Evan James of Pontypridd, the tune being composed by his son, James James, but one tradition maintains that the son composed the music and then asked his father to provide appropriate words.

The song was probably sung publicly for the first time in 1856 in a chapel in Maesteg, Glamorgan. It was sung in the Aberystwyth National Eisteddfod in 1865 and in the Bangor National Eisteddfod in 1874, when it began to assume a 'national' flavour. It was sung by Eos Morlais (see page 134) whose rendering took the eisteddfod by storm.

But many feel today that it is not worthy of its mantle.They are uneasy with these warlike words that refer to the blood of the (fictional?) brave, patriotic Welsh soldier being shed on the battlefield in the cause of 'freedom': 'Ein gwrol ryfelwyr, gwladgarwyr tra mad. Tros ryddid collasant eu gwaed'.

One or two words can cause problems to many. For example, the penultimate line reads:

> Tra môr yn fur i'r bur hoff bau . . .

The last word, pau, mutated (bau) is an obsolete word for country. It offers a 'prayer' for the language to remain alive whilst the sea (môr) continues as a wall (mur) to the pure (pur, mutated—bur), hoff (loved) country.

You will know that 'wlad' is the mutated form of 'gwlad'. In the soft mutation the letter 'g' is usually dropped, but it is usually retained in borrowed words like 'gêm' or 'golff', as they sound a bit silly mutated. For example: Hoffech chi (would you like) êm o olff? You will hardly ever find a mutated form of grŵp (from the English, group).

The same melody is used in the National Anthem of Brittany and it is suggested by a few that it borrows rather heavily from an English melody, 'Old Rosin the Beau'.

15

Being royal can be better than being Welsh

The University of Wales celebrated its centenary in 1993, but there are a few who feel that it has outlived its purpose and that it should be dismantled, thus solving many organisational and financing problems.

It all started in Aberystwyth. It was there in 1872 that the first constituent college of the university was established, one of its main tasks being to teach the sons of Wales to express themselves in the English tongue and think British. They did not think that 'Welsh' would be an appropriate subject for the timetable, nor did they think that this omission would ignite any protests.

There are many who feel that Aberystwyth college (and the others that followed) have performed their task remarkably well. This (for example) may be seen in a desire to go to royalty for the names of certain hospitals as they are considered more appropriate than names rooted in Wales. It is rumoured that the Polytechnic of Wales at one time thought that the University of a certain princess would be a good name for it. The name ultimately adopted was the University of Glamorgan, or Prifysgol Morgannwg as they finally thought that 'Morgan' would be more appropriate than 'Diana'.

'Than' and 'nor' have very similar ultimate consonants in Welsh that can confuse the ear. 'Than' is 'nag' and 'nor' is 'nac' which often becomes 'nag' in conversation.

'Na(g)' is used (for example) after a comparative adjective. We might say, 'Mae mwy (comparative of 'mawr' = big) yma heddiw nag arfer' or 'Mae mwy yma (heddiw) na ddoe'. We use 'nag' before a vowel. We might say, in another context, 'Does dim arian nac amser gen i', or 'Does dim arian na bwyd gen i yn y tŷ'. Here the 'c' is dropped before a consonant. But people usually say, 'Does dim arian nag amser gen i', softening the consonant; hence the confusion. You may use 'na(c)' before a number of nouns, thus: 'Does dim arian nac amser nac amynedd nac esgus gen i chwaith'.

To return to 'nag', you might say, 'Mae Gwen yn dewach nag Elin, ond yn deneuach nag Olwen', or 'Mae Morgan yn well nag (yw) Diana'.

Coleg Prifysgol Cymru, Aberystwyth

Travelling from Siapan to Siohn o'Groats

People have been suggesting that Welsh place-names should be regenerated; for example, such a suggestion was made in Ferndale, in Rhondda valley a few years ago. At one time, Ferndale was referred to as Glynrhedyn, but this name is not mentioned in A *Gazetteer of Welsh Place-Names*.

Welsh place-names can be lost and eroded in many ways. Sometimes, English speakers who find pronouncing Welsh place-names difficult are to blame. They 'adjust' a name and this adjustment takes root.

Landore in Swansea is an English corruption of 'Glan-dŵr' (water's edge). Just outside Cardiff, there is a village referred to in English as Pendoylan, the Welsh being Pendeulwyn (the end of two bushes). A few of these Welsh place-names are beautiful, for example Allt-yr-ynn in Newport. What you will hear, however, is Altereen. You have Manacles in Cornwall, a corruption of 'Maneglwys' (church place) and the famous post office transmitting station in Cornwall, Goonhilly Downs is a corruption of 'Gwaunhela' (hunting field).

Basaleg near Newport derives from the Latin *basilica* and has an historical interest, but English speakers refer to the place as 'base leg'. Penychain (the head of oxen) near Caernarfon is pronounced in English as Penny Chain.

Welsh speakers often ignore the letter J and you will not find it in many alphabets. It occurs in borrowed words like jam. There is a tendency also to ignore it when referring to Japan. A few seem to prefer Siapan.

Yr Atlas Cymraeg, has attempted to solve this problem. It has Japan, and you will note that you can go to Jamaica and Jersey and Jerusalem without encountering the 'si' problem. The atlas attempts also to eradicate the habit of using the definite article in front of certain place/country names. You can say, 'Rwy'n mynd i Ariannin' (not Yr Ariannin) and you are welcome in 'Iwerddon' and not 'Yr Iwerddon', or 'India' and not 'Yr India'.

Nearer home go to Amwythig (Shrewsbury) and not Yr Amwythig, but you have to go to Yr Almaen (Germany) and Yr Aifft (Egypt). But if you feel like a long walk, do not go to Siohn O'Groats.

Don't be swallowed by the dentist

Under a thousand copies of the first Christmas card were printed in 1843. They retailed at one shilling (5p) each. Every year in recent times, we in Britain post enough cards to go, end to end, more than twice around the world.

And with the shops open on Sundays we will have much more time in which to purchase them. The postman will do the rest.

Those who are against shopping on Sundays often say that they are defending our 'traditional day of rest' but 'traditional' can mean different things to different people. Traditionally in Wales, even Christmas Day was hardly a holy day. After attending a morning service, many parishes would organise rough and tumble football matches, the games being devoid of rules, and often lasting until dark. Hunting was also popular.

But talking of sending cards to friends and relatives and of going to the shops can present a linguistic problem to the unwary. The trap lies in the preposition 'to'. 'Rwy'n mynd i'r siop nawr', could translate, 'I'm going to the shop now', the 'to the' translating into 'i'r'. But if you wish to say, 'I'm sending a Christmas card to Mother', it would be wrong to say in Welsh, 'Rwy'n anfon cerdyn Nadolig i Mam'. To be strictly correct, you should say, 'Rwy'n anfon cerdyn Nadolig at Mam'.

This subtle difference is important. If you wish to say that you are going to the house, you say, 'Rwy'n mynd i'r tŷ', but if you have severe indigestion after eating too much turkey, and wish to go to the doctor, you say in Welsh, 'Rwy'n mynd at y meddyg'.

Saying, 'Mynd i'r meddyg', implies that the doctor is in the process of swallowing you. Similarly, say, 'Rwy'n mynd at y deintydd' (dentist), or 'Rwy'n mynd i'r car at Mam'. It's 'at' to a person and 'i' to a place. A tradition that should be maintained.

Who, which and what with books

If you read the *Annual Reports* of the Welsh Books Council you will discover how far book publishing in Wales has progressed since the Council was established in the early sixties. Every year it offers financial support to around 200 books by over 20 different publishers.

No other minority language has such a unique body to promote the production of books. But there are many who feel that it is difficult to publish anything in Wales that is not supported by the Council. They are uneasy about the apparent monopoly that has developed, but they should be more uneasy about the fact that fewer and fewer people read books nowadays.

At any time of the year it is difficult to think of a better present than a book. The variety of titles on offer, both for children and adults, might well surprise you. But be careful when you consult your bookseller in Welsh.

A problem could lie with two simple words that can cause confusion. They are 'pa' and 'pwy'.

When you ask a question, 'pa' means 'what' or 'which' and 'pwy' (generally) means 'who'.

'Pwy' is an often used word. You might ask, 'Pwy sy 'na?' when you hear a noise in the house. You might also ask your bookseller, 'Pwy sgrifennodd y llyfr yma?'

You may also wish to compare three books and ask, 'Which book is the best?' This translates simply, 'Pa lyfr yw'r gore?'

Nothing should be simpler. But many Welsh speakers ignore 'pa' in conversation and you might well hear someone ask, 'Pwy lyfr yw'r gore?' or, 'Pwy gyhoeddwyr sy'n cyhoeddi'r llyfr?'

Media presenters often do this. On record programmes, they often ask, 'Pwy gân/record ych chi eisie?' Whilst many of us would prefer, 'Pa gân/record . . .' we have to accept that this is just an example of a thriving language.

But there are instances when both words are not interchangeable. It is this which causes the confusion.

For England, read Wales

A few years ago, the Welsh Rugby Union described its newly designed playing kit as 'sensational, full of colour'. Until public opinion caused a change of mind, the Union had decided to use 'Wales' instead of 'Cymru' on this particular kit.

The Saxons used to describe the Welsh as 'foreigners' and the country as Wales, 'the foreign land', so, as the Union now aims to encourage non-Welsh players to play in the Welsh team, its initial preference for 'Wales' is understandable.

The Britons of the 'Wales' of many moons ago preferred to call themselves 'Cymry', the plural of Cymro, a compound of 'com', a prefix meaning 'together' and 'bro', meaning 'border, coast or district'. Cumberland, in the north of England, means 'the land of the Cymry'. At one time, the people of Cumberland would be conversant with Cymraeg (Welsh), the language of the Cymry.

There was a time when Cymry was used to describe the people and the country, but later, in order to differentiate, the name of the land was spelt with an 'u' and we now have 'Cymru'.

We also differentiate between the language, Cymraeg (Welsh, in Welsh) and Cymreig (pertaining to Wales), but the line between both can sometimes be tenuous and confusing (see page 163). People often say 'Cymraeg' when they should say 'Cymreig'. There are certain areas of Wales where Welsh is the dominant language. We describe such an area as 'y fro Gymraeg'. This means, 'the district where Welsh is spoken'. If you live in such an area, you would say, 'Rwy'n byw mewn bro Gymraeg' (I live in a Welsh-speaking district).

The Welsh for The Welsh Office is 'Y Swyddfa Gymreig'. It is wrong to say, 'Rwy'n gweithio yn y Swyddfa Gymraeg' (I'm working in the Welsh (speaking) Office). Hardly any Welsh is spoken there. In Welsh you would say, 'Does dim llawer o Gymraeg yn y Swyddfa Gymreig'. Should we wish to be pedantic we could say that the English rugby fifteen comes from 'Wales'. Linguistically speaking, who are the 'foreigners'?

Clean sheets, new pennies and old men

New Year's Day in Wales used to be much more significant than Christmas Day. 'Talu hen ddyledion' (paying old debts) before that day was important so that the new year would begin with a clean sheet. It was considered unlucky to lend anything to anyone on New Year's Day. People would try to get up at the crack of dawn, or 'gyda'r ceiliog' (with the cockerel) as this would be setting the standard for the rest of the year.

One custom, which is almost extinct, was that of collecting the 'calennig' (New Year's Gift). Children all over rural Wales used to walk (or run) from house to house, and receive a 'ceiniog newydd' for chanting 'Blwyddyn Newydd Dda'. The gift would sometimes be food, like fruit and cakes, placed in a bag carried for that purpose. They had to stop at twelve noon as the year had lost its newness by then.

English cannot always be used as a guide when attempting to understand a Welsh phrase or sentence. 'Blwyddyn Newydd Dda' is not a translation of 'Happy New Year'. 'Blwyddyn' is 'year' and 'newydd' is 'new' but the English 'happy' is 'hapus' in Welsh. 'Dda' (mutated here) means 'good'.

Note also the position of the adjective in relation to the word which it describes. In Welsh, the adjective almost always comes after a noun, for example, 'Mae ceiniog newydd gen i'.

An important exception is 'hen' (old), as in 'old debts' above (see also page 172). In Welsh, we say 'yr hen flwyddyn' for 'the old year'. There is a subtle difference between 'Mae'n hen ddyn' (He is an old man) and 'Mae'n ddyn hen' which would translate roughly as 'He is a really old man'.

Both young and old must have a finely tuned ear when learning a language. Note that 'ceiniog' has an 'n' in the middle, but 'ceiliog' has an 'l'. Look after the consonants, and the vowels will look after themselves.

A look at a murderer's accomplice

Curnow Vosper's painting, *Salem,* depicting a chapel in Cwm Nantcol, near Llanbedr, Harlech is well known in Wales and over the years legends have grown around it. The most interesting one involves the devil.

The painting was painted in 1908, and it depicts villagers in prayer and Siân Owen, a colourful shawl over her shoulders, walking to her pew. A bilingual book about the painting (written by Tal Williams) was published a few years ago by Barddas. In it, the author seeks to disentangle fact from fiction.

The most famous legend says that Siân Owen had sinned and that the devil has revealed himself/herself in the folds of her shawl. The artist maintained that this was purely accidental, but people have insisted over the years that they can see him. It seems that certain people have such a close acquaintance with the evil one that they know what he/she looks like.

Which brings me to a particular aspect of evil in our midst.

Reporting on a murder recently, a media newscaster said, 'Trywanodd y ferch gyda chyllell'. (He stabbed the girl with a knife).

Grammatically speaking, his statement was not strictly correct. He had been misled by a very hard working one-letter word in Welsh, 'a'.

This word can have many meanings as it stands. If it is circumflexed, it has still other meanings, one of which being 'gyda' (with). I mention on page 26 how this word is being misused in Welsh. In this particular example, 'â' denotes an object and 'gyda' denotes company. Grammatically speaking, therefore, the news-reader stated that the murderer (accompanied by a knife) had stabbed the girl. To be strictly correct, he should have said, 'Trywanodd y ferch â chyllell'.

Should you wish to ask someone, 'What are you writing with?' you would say, 'Â beth wyt ti'n sgrifennu?' (Not: 'Gyda beth wyt ti'n sgrifennu?').

Murdering this particular rule is of no great consequence, but it is just as well for you to know that many people still use 'â' rather than 'gyda' in conversation to denote an object.

Knowing a way around books and people

Those travelling to Aberystwyth from the south cannot fail to see and recognise the National Library of Wales. It is an imposing edifice on Penglais Hill, a comfortable walk of one mile from the town centre. It is a copyright library and therefore, as a custodian of the nation's treasures, it has a right to a free copy of every book and periodical published in Great Britain and the Republic of Ireland.

If you are over eighteen years of age you may have a reader's ticket (provided a request for one is signed by a person of recognised standing who knows you well) and may go there to read all these books and periodicals at your leisure.

In theory, at least. It would take years for you to read through a few of the shelves, and it might be useful to know that you cannot borrow them to take home with you.

'To know' can translate into 'adnabod' or 'gwybod' in Welsh. 'To recognise' can also mean 'adnabod' and this can cause confusion at times. In conversation, if you wish to know if a friend knows somebody, you could well ask, quite incorrectly, 'Ydych chi'n gwybod y llyfrgellydd?' But though this could translate as 'Do you know the librarian?' it will sound most odd to a first-language speaker.

When you refer to a person, you must always use 'adnabod', and you would have to say, 'Dw i ddim yn (ad)nabod y llyfrgellydd'. As the brackets in the previous sentence indicate, in conversation, 'adnabod' is often shortened to 'nabod'.

But if you wish to ask about the whereabouts of the library, you should ask, 'Ydych chi'n gw(y)bod ble mae'r llyfrgell?' The full negative response might be, 'Dw i ddim yn gwybod'.

'Rwy'n (ad)nabod rhywun sy'n gw(y)bod y ffordd i'r llyfrgell', would translate, 'I know somebody who knows the way to the library'.

Briefly, use 'adnabod' for persons. But if someone tells you, 'Rwy'n adnabod rhywun sy'n gwybod am bob llyfr yn y llyfrgell', tell him that you know differently.

Llyfrgell Genedlaethol Cymru, Aberystwyth

To have a passport may lack validity

Many groups have been set up to assist in the promotion of the Welsh language. One such group is 'Cefn'. One of its aims is to secure equal validity for the language in business. Not so very long ago, an official from the Passport Office in Liverpool informed this organisation that it was 'not unreasonable' for a passport applicant to fill an English-language application form.

A Cefn official from Caernarfon who had applied for a passport had supplied him with a professionally translated form, but he was not happy with this arrangement. Apparently, it had no validity.

The preposition 'with' can cause problems in Welsh. We have at least two words for 'with', namely 'gan' and 'gyda'. Grammatically speaking, 'gyda' denotes company and 'gan' denotes an agent or operator, but the dividing line between the two shades of meaning is being eroded constantly. As they are so similar, language learners have been advised to forget about 'gan' until they become more proficient in the language and to use 'gyda' at all times.

A Welsh speaker, fully aware of the rule, would say, 'Mae llawer o ffrindiau gyda Gwyn', but, 'Mae llawer o arian gan Olwen'. We do not always say 'gyda'. We tend to drop the 'gy' and we would say, 'Does dim llawer o ffrindiau 'da hi'.

As you would be understood anyway, and as many of us seem to be breaking this minor rule, you may stick to 'gyda' but you should be aware of the meaning of 'gan'.

The rule is less likely to be broken in standardised written Welsh and Welsh purists would never say, 'Mae llawer o waith 'da (or gyda) fi'. They would say, 'Mae llawer o waith gen i' (see page 23).

But in Caernarfon, 'gyda' does not have much validity. They would use 'efo' instead and say, 'Does dim pasbort efo Gwyn'. Remember, efo = gyda, and is much used in north Wales; a further example of the richness of the language.

Boys and girls on St Dwynwen's island

January 25 is an important day in the calendar of those whose thoughts are turning to love. This is when St Dwynwen's Day is celebrated, Dwynwen being the patron saint of Welsh sweethearts. According to tradition, Dwynwen's boyfriend wished to ravish her outside the bonds of marriage. She resisted his advances and fled (with the help of God) from mid Wales to Anglesey. She was sanctified and built a church on Llanddwyn Island, the remains of which can still be seen. For years young couples used to go on pilgrimages to Anglesey and would make a lovers' wish by Dwynwen's well. Many in Wales would like this custom revived, as Dwynwen's story is much more romantic than that of St Valentine.

Which brings me to one of the most difficult problems that beset learners; that of determining the gender of a noun. All nouns can be either masculine or feminine in Welsh; there is no neuter gender. For the most part the gender of particular nouns must be learnt. Guidelines can help. It is inappropriate to say 'rules' in this respect as they can be subject to many exceptions.

More often than not, nouns that end in '-es' are feminine. Many are formed from the masculine. Therefore, we have 'sant' becoming 'santes'. We would say of Dwynwen, 'Mae eglwys y santes hon ym Môn'.

But many nouns end in '-es' anyway. We might ask of a televised series, 'Ydy'r gyfres hon wedi gorffen?' One important exception is 'hanes' and we would say, 'Mae'r hanes hwn yn ddiddorol'.

Nouns ending in '-en' are usually feminine and we would say, 'Mae'r daten hon yn boeth', or 'Ydy'r goeden hon yn hen?' An important exception here is 'bachgen'. We would say, 'Mae'r bachgen a'r ferch ger ffynnon Dwynwen', but 'Mae'r ferch a'r bachgen ger ffynnon Dwynwen', 'merch' being mutated.

You will be aware that there is a close link between genders and mutating, that is why commiting them to memory is so important.

It is wise to say 'no' the first time

One of the problems facing the government in 1995 was whether Great Britain, as a member of the European Community, should forgo British currency and say 'yes' to a common currency in the near future. One Conservative party leader stated as a reason for saying 'no', that 'We do not wish to be governed by those who do not speak our language'.

Many of us smile rather sadly whilst we recall such a remark. We in Wales are quite used to this.

It can be rather difficult for us to say 'no' in conversation as the form of the negative depends on the structure of the question. If you wish to reply in the negative to the question, 'Oes amser gen ti?' the answer is 'Nac oes' (pronounced 'nag oes'). You simply say the first word of the question after 'nac'.

If you are asked, 'Wyt ti'n dod heno?' you might reply, 'Nac ydw', a slight difference. But if you are asked, 'Fyddi di'n dod heno?' your answer would be 'Na fydda(f)', Here, the 'c' in 'nac' is dropped before a consonant.

To complicate things still more, if you are asked, '(Ai) ti wnaeth e?' the negative answer is, 'Nage'. This occurs if the question begins with 'Ai', a word that is often omitted from the beginning of a query. Welsh speakers often go a step further and say, 'Nage ddim'.

To take things still further, if you are asked, 'Wnest ti e?' the answer is 'Naddo'. This happens in the past or perfect tenses. Here again, you might encounter, 'Naddo ddim'.

But you can say 'no' in a much simpler way as you master these complexities. Just say 'Na'. In a way this reflects the English 'No'.

Discovering America and all that

In the autumn of 1992, the Americans celebrated the fifth centenary of the discovery of their country by Christopher Columbus. When he set sail from Spain in 1492 in the hope of discovering a new route to China, he was in the habit of calling himself Admiral Christobal Colô'n. He would not have answered to the name Christopher Columbus. We in Wales would not dream of joining such celebrations as the true discoverer of America was Madog the son of Owain Gwynedd. He landed in Mobile Bay in the Gulf of Mexico in 1170. The good people of Alabama have erected a tablet to commemorate the fact.

We may conveniently forget that the Scandinavian countries would say that Eric the Red landed in Vinland in 1002, but perhaps we should bear in mind that the Germans, the Chinese, the French, and even the English, amongst others, have their own 'true' tale of the discovery of 'the new world'.

Perhaps it would have been better for the Americans in 1992 to have commemorated the fact that nobody knows who discovered their continent, despite the fact that Madog is reputed to have taught Welsh to the Mandan Indians (see page 200).

Learners could well find it difficult to understand someone who says 'I don't know' in Welsh. They might have been taught to say, 'Dydw i ddim yn gwybod', or 'Dwy i ddim yn gw(y)bod', both syntactically sound sentences, but many indigenous Welsh speakers might use more colloquial forms. You might hear a person say, 'Sa i'n gw'bod', 'So i'n gw'pod', 'Smo i'n gw'bod', 'Wn i ddim' (or 'Wn i'm'), depending upon which part of the country the speaker hails from.

A few speakers have eroded 'Dydw i ddim yn gwybod' over the years more than any other phrase. If they wish to plead ignorance in conversation, they might well take the last letter of the third word (ddim) and the fourth and fifth letters of the last word (gwybod) and get an 'm' followed by 'bo'. Finely tune your ears after asking a knowledgeable Welshman who discovered America and you might hear, 'M bo'. You can't prune further that that.

A magazine for women and some affirmative treason

On 23 February 1852 a famous Welshman died in Cardiff when he was a few months short of his 31st birthday. You will find his grave in the cemetery of Groes-wen chapel, Caerffili. His name was Evan Jones, but people will always remember him as Ieuan Gwynedd, a minister and a journalist. One of his most famous publications was the pioneering *Y Gymraes* that he subtitled as 'cylchgrawn i ferched Cymru', but his most important work as a journalist was a campaign against a report by English commissioners on education in Wales published in blue covered books in 1847. Ieuan Gwynedd and others branded this report as 'brad y llyfrau gleision' (treachery of the blue books) (see page 53). The commissioners stated (amongst other pontifications) that Welsh was a 'peculiar language isolating the masses from the upper portion of society'. After such criticism many of these masses opted to say 'yes' to an education in the English tongue, despite the efforts of Ieuan Gwynedd and others.

It can be quite difficult for a learner to say 'yes' in Welsh. When confronted with a plethora of means of doing so, his instinct might be to think of 'yes' and say 'ie'. But this shot in the dark is often wrong. One of the most common of these affirmative forms is 'ydy', shortened from 'ydyw'. You may hear an echo of the required response here in a possible question in a garage, 'Ydy'r car yn barod?' If the car is ready, the response will be 'ydy', but this may not always be the case.

In some areas, people might say 'ody' or even 'oty'. North Walians are not happy with the grammatically correct spelling as they utter the ultimate 'y' less gutturally and they favour the written form 'ydi', but remember that 'ydy', 'ody', 'ydi' and 'oti' all mean 'yes'.

Many people today do not follow this rule. If a person is asked, for example, 'Ydy e wedi ca'l brecwast?' he might well answer, 'do'. 'Do' is the correct response to, 'Fuest ti yn y dosbarth neithiwr?' but it is not a response to use in instances such as, 'Ych chi wedi gorffen?' or 'Ydy e wedi mynd?' But you will hear these wrong answers often. Look upon the response as a tiny bit of grammatical treason that is gaining popularity.

Y Ddraig Goch ddyry cychwyn

Tradition maintains that Saint David died on 1 March; that is why this date is celebrated as St David's Day. (Dydd Gŵyl Ddewi or Dydd Gŵyl Dewi). The Welsh flag is often flown over public buildings for this one day in our calendar. It is then refurled and returned to its cupboard until the next St David's Day. The banners of Ireland and Scotland are incorporated in the flag of the United Kingdom, the Union Jack. The Welsh Dragon is the only flag that is not represented on it. But it is much older than the Union Jack. It flew over Bosworth field when Harri Tewdwr/Tudur (Henry Tudor) defeated King Richard III in 1485.

The dragon is often displayed on patriotic emblems, sometimes accompanied by the slogan: 'Y Ddraig Goch ddyry cychwyn', the strictly correct version. You might well see 'Y Ddraig Goch a ddyry gychwyn'. Both mean, 'The Red Dragon leads the way', but there is no need for the pronoun before 'ddyry', nor should 'cychwyn' be mutated.

People often say, erroneously, 'Y Ddraig Goch ddaru gychwyn' (It was the Red Dragon that started (it all)). They could well have been misled by our use of auxiliary verbs. This avoids the necessity of using the verb noun when expressing the tense of a verb.

'Ddaru' is a colloquial verb used mainly in north Wales, and is the past tense, third person singular, of the verb noun 'gwneud'. The more commonly used form is 'gwnaeth' which means, 'he (or she) did'. People often feel that, 'Dewi wnaeth gychwyn' slips easier off the tongue than, 'Dewi gychwynnodd', but you might hear the more colloquial form, 'Dewi 'na'th gychwyn' in conversation.

The first sentence of this article begs a question. 'Is it "Gŵyl Dewi" or "Gŵyl Ddewi"?' You may take your choice. If you translate it as 'The Festival of David', it should be "Gŵyl Ddewi" but if you wish to consider that the personal noun 'Dewi' operates as an adjective, do not mutate. There are many who feel that the name of our patron saint should not be mutated.

Welsh prohibited—by order!

Young Owen M Edwards, from a homestead outside Llanuwchllyn in Gwynedd, was informed by his headteacher, when he first attended school in 1858, that Welsh, his only language, was prohibited. Any child breaking this rule was required to carry a wooden tag, with WN (Welsh Not) on it, around his neck. The wearer at the end of the day would be punished. Such an injustice caused young Owen to rebel. He grew up to be the most important and influential Welsh benefactor of his day and was able to undertake much to eradicate the stigma of the Welsh Not. His publications in Welsh were numerous, and in January 1892 he published a magazine called *Cymru'r Plant*. (The Wales of the Children). It was full of good articles and yarns. In 1992, the centenary of this publication was celebrated, but the famous (and good) title had been replaced by something more 'with it' a few years before.

'Good' is a word that has to work hard in Welsh. You come across it early when you learn the greetings, 'Bore da', 'Pnawn da', 'Dydd da', or 'Nos da'. 'Bore', 'pnawn' and 'dydd' take the masculine gender, and the adjective 'da' is not mutated after them. 'Nos' takes the feminine gender, but 'da' is not mutated after it, as you might expect; but if you use 'noswaith' (evening)—which is feminine, 'da' takes the soft mutation after it and you say, 'noswaith dda'.

But 'da' can also mean 'cows' in many parts of south Wales. 'Maen nhw'n godro'r da', means that they are milking the cows. 'Da pluog' (literally 'feathered goods') is used to describe poultry, as 'da' can also refer to 'goods'.

If a person is unwell, he might say, 'Dydw i ddim yn dda'. You will know that 'Da iawn, diolch', means 'Very well, thank you'. If somebody plays a good game, we would say, 'Mae'n chwarae'n dda', or you might hear, 'Ma' fe'n whare'n dda'.

'Mae'r bachgen da'n trin y da'n dda', would mean, 'The good boy treats the cows well', but don't worry, you would never be required to say such a sentence.

Owen Morgan Edwards

Orenjis, grêps, and what have you

Around a century ago, the people of Wales seemed to be more familiar with the geography of Palestine than that of Wales. Today, a person studying the names of chapels will become aware that the 'promised land' is the source of most of them. Names like Bethel, Bethlehem, Carmel, Jerwsalem, Moriah and Tabor abound. Sometimes they have spilt over and have become names of villages like Adpar and Bethesda.

Farmers often paid more attention to the rotation of crops in the Garden of Eden than in their own backyards, possibly blaming that famous apple for their toils. But the apple can plead innocence as there is no reference to apples in that particular horticultural paradise. Though it is a much maligned fruit learners could enter a greengrocer's shop in Wales before metrication and ask for 'pwys o fale' and cause no consternation.

The correct word for 'apples' is 'afalau'. In north Wales, you may expect to hear 'fala'. It is the only fruit that has retained its Welshness over the years. Learners must become used to Welsh speakers choosing to use English words for fruit whilst perfectly good ones still abound.

There is a strong movement these days to get the major stores to use Welsh over their counters. This could well provide a backlash. For example, the sign 'Bricyll—hanner can ceiniog y pwys' (Apricots—50p per pound) could cause consternation to many a Welsh speaker who might be happier with 'Apricots, ffiffti pee y pownd'. Hardly anybody these days uses 'bricyll', but stores could before long be displaying, 'Grawnwin melys, orenau, mefus, mafon, eirin gwlanog ac eirin Mair' for grapes, oranges, strawberries, raspberries, peaches and gooseberries.

The strawberry can present a problem. It is known in areas of south Wales as 'syfïen'. It might be safer to stick to bananas. But have you ever tried 'cloron'?

Goats—again, again and yet again

One of the most famous songs in the repertoire of male voice choirs is 'Cyfri'r geifr' (Counting the goats). The choir asks plaintively, 'Oes gafr eto?' and this elicits the reply, 'Oes, heb ei godro'. The goat could well be black, white, red, blue or even pink, but beware, the Welsh names for these colours are mutated, and could cause confusion.

This is an old 'nonsense' cumulative folk song, composed most probably as a tongue twister and a bit of fun, but note that the initial 'oes' in the question, elicits the positive response, 'oes', that is, the clue for the 'yes' is in the question itself. You could ask, '(A) oes gwers heno?' and have the affirmative reply, 'Oes'. The negative response would be 'Nac oes' (pronounced 'nag oes').

But let us look at the word 'eto' in the same question. With verbs in the present and future tense (as in this inquiry about unmilked goats) we know that it means 'again'. Indeed, you could say 'eto, plîs/unwaith eto, plîs' instead of saying 'I beg your pardon', when you ask for a remark to be repeated.

But if the verb is in the present perfect tense, 'eto' means 'yet', and you might say, 'Dwy'i ddim wedi gorffen eto'. Sometimes, the initial 'e' of 'eto' is dropped in conversation, and what you hear is ''to'.

With verbs in the past tense, use 'unwaith eto' if you wish to express 'once again', for example, 'Es i'r banc unwaith eto' (I went to the bank once again). In this instance, you could use another word, 'drachefn' for 'once again', in a sentence such as, 'Mi es i fyny i'r mynydd drachefn a thrachefn' (note the mutation here).

But not to look for pink goats, please.

Vote for a woman, if there is one

Women often complain that they cannot vote for women in general elections. It is also difficult for a woman to be selected to stand. In 1995 Wales had only one woman Member of Parliament, Mrs Ann Clwyd in the Cynon valley.

One of the most remarkable women born in Wales, and one who surmounted many odds against women was Amy Dilwyn of Swansea who was born in 1845. She was one of the earliest supporters of the National Union of Women's Suffrage Societies. She took over the almost bankrupt Llansamlet Spelter Works after her father's death and converted it into a commercial success. She could often be seen smoking cigars in public on her way to work. She was 90 when she died.

This brings me once again to the question of gender. It can be time consuming to attempt to master the gender of nouns in Welsh. The best way by far is to listen to broadcasters and people talking. Reading will also help.

Listen for mutations, the form of the numeral or the form of the demonstrative pronoun. For example, hearing someone say, 'marchnad fawr', 'dwy stori', or 'y ganrif hon', will make you aware that you are amongst feminine nouns. On the other hand, 'dau bennill', 'trwyn mawr', and 'y mis hwn', will tell you that you are amongst masculine nouns. Unfortunately, there can be discrepancies and many people in north Wales would say 'dwy bennill'.

The names of days, months and seasons are always masculine. You would say, 'Doedd y gaeaf hwn ddim yn oer', or 'Mae dau ddiwrnod cyn dydd Mawrth', or, 'Rydw i'n hoffi Mehefin poeth'. But you must say, 'y flwyddyn hon'.

There are many nouns which end in '-ad'. They are nearly all masculine but two common ones are feminine and you would have to say, 'Mae pedwar llygad gan ddwy ddafad', or 'Mae llawer o fynyddoedd yn y wlad hon'.

Words that end in '-yn', '-cyn' and '-wr' are usually masculine, but you could be caught by one or two exceptions. I have already referred to 'blwyddyn' (year). 'Telyn' (harp) is also feminine, but to be strictly correct, the '-yn' in both these examples are not endings.

Women may not be pleased to know that it is usual for newly devised technical terms to be masculine. This is a policy to avoid possible mutating problems as there are more mutations in feminine than in masculine forms.

Wishing for a bit of home rule can make you ill

More and more countries seem to be clamouring for home rule these days but such a demand is nothing new in Wales and Lloyd George, the Welsh-speaking prime minister, was a strong exponent of home rule at one time. In fine oratorical style, he developed his argument in parliament one day. He referred to numerous countries as being worthy of home rule and drew enormous cheers. He then came to his climax and exclaimed, 'Home Rule for Wales'. One member heckled angrily, 'Home Rule for Hell!' 'Quite right. Every man for his own country!' was his reply, which makes many wish that the practice of heckling would return to the hustings.

Such a wish brings me to a small word that is often misused in one context these days, namely, 'am'. It is often used simply to express a wish, for example, 'Rydw i am fynd adre cyn swper', or a query, 'Ych chi am ragor o de?'

Nothing could be simpler, but these days it is often used to refer to the 'wish' of an inanimate object. You may hear a news-reader say on the media, 'Mae'r ffordd osgoi am gychwyn yn y gwanwyn', or, 'Mae'r gwylie am ddechre fory'.

A correct sentence would be, 'Bydd y gwaith ar y ffordd osgoi yn cychwyn yn y gwanwyn', but this does not slip as easily off the tongue and the incorrect expression is gaining in popularity.

You might hear a person say, 'Dw i am fod yn sâl, dw i'n meddwl', which translates, 'I wish to be ill, I think'. The statement here should have been, 'Dw i'n mynd i fod yn sâl, dw i'n meddwl'.

This again is a more involved (but correct) structure but many speakers cut corners and ignore correct grammar in order to express themselves by the shortest means possible and though it might make you ill to hear a misused 'am', you must live with it.

Always look for the best

If folklore is to be believed, the best runner the world has ever seen was Griffith Morgan from Nyth-brân in the parish of Llanwynno by Pontypridd. He died when he was 37 after he had just won a race against an Englishman. This was from the centre of Newport to Bedwas church near Caerffili, a distance of 12 miles. If you think that there is nothing remarkable in this, I should mention that Griffith (or Guto Nyth Brân as he was called) ran, whilst the Englishman was on horseback. He ran this particular race in 53 minutes, an average of 4.4 minutes per mile; proof that he was indeed the best.

The Welsh word for 'best' is 'gorau' and is made to work as hard as Guto. It is the superlative form of the adjective 'da' and you will be familiar with it in phrases like 'bore da' and 'noswaith dda'.

The translation for 'He was the best' would be 'Fe oedd y gorau', but it may also be used in a plural form, 'goreuon'. 'Nhw yw'r goreuon', would be 'They are the best'.

You should also familiarise yourself with one or two idioms in which it appears. If we wish to undertake a task at once, we say, 'Gorau po gyntaf'. This translates roughly as 'Sooner the better'.

If we wish to ask someone to stop teasing, we would say, 'Rho'r gorau (gore) iddi hi'. This example shows how futile it often is to ask for a literal English translation. Roughly and nonsensically this could be, 'Give the best to her'. If we wished to say that someone had given of his best in a race, we would say, 'Roedd e ar 'i ore yn y ras'.

If we agree to undertake a task, we would say, 'O'r gore', roughly equivalent to O.K. (All right).

Returning to Guto, we could say, 'Roedd ar 'i ore mewn ras'. Perhaps I should add that he died of heart failure after his girlfriend had given him a hefty congratulatory pat on the back. The moral? Don't follow women and horses.

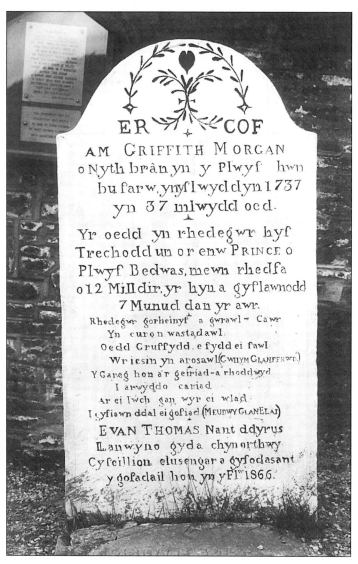

ER ✠ COF

AM GRIFFITH MORGAN
o Nyth brân yn y Plwyf hwn
bu farw, ynyflwyddyn 1737
yn 37 mlwydd oed.

Yr oedd yn rhedegwr hyf
Trechodd un or enw PRINCE o
Plwyf Bedwas, mewn rhedfa
o 12 Milldir, yr hyn a gyflawnodd
7 Munud dan yr awr.

Rhedegwr gorheinyf a gwrawl — Cawr
Yn curon wastadawl.
Oedd Gruffydd, e fydd ei fawl
Wr iesin yn arosawl (GWILYM GLANFFRWD.)
Y Garreg hon a'r geiriad-a rhoddwyd
I arwyddo cariad.
Ar ei lwch gan wyr ei wlad:
I gyfiawn ddal ei gofiad (MEUDWY GLANELAI)

EVAN THOMAS Nant ddyrus
Llanwyno gyda chynorthwy
Cyfeillion elusengar a gyfodasant
y gofadail hon yn y Fl. 1866.

Bedd Guto Nyth Brân ym mynwent Llanwynno

Always eat and drink loads at the right times

In the fifteenth century, a gentleman called Rhys ap Maredudd in south Ceredigion was famous for his magnificent feasts. A poet of that time, Dafydd Nanmor, described such a feast for us. In one section of his poem (a cywydd) he maintains that if all the earth were bread, and if all water tasted like fine wine, and if three hundred vineyards produced wine for him and if there were a hundred mills milling flour, the product of such diligence would all be consumed in three days.

You may take that description of a meal with the proverbial pinch of salt, but even so, be wary at mealtimes. The Welsh for 'meal times' is 'prydau bwyd', the plural for 'pryd bwyd' because we also refer to 'times' generally, but with a different plural form, 'prydiau', with an 'i' added. You might find that supermarkets sometimes err in this respect when offering Welsh language translations. When they offer 'prydau parod' (prepared meals) as part of their fare, they should never offer 'prydiau parod', as this translates as 'ready times'.

The word 'pryd' is much used in more than one way and I offer a few examples only. If you wish to ask someone when he/she is going, you might ask, 'Pryd wyt ti'n mynd?' If someone has overstayed his/her welcome, you could suggest tersely, 'Mae'n bryd i ti fynd'. If you are annoyed with a person, give him/her a taste of your tongue, or 'pryd o dafod'. If someone comes just in time, you could say, 'Rwyt ti wedi cyrraedd mewn pryd'. If he came before time, you could say, 'Fe ddest ti mewn da bryd' (. . . in good time). If you wish to say that you go out to have a meal from time to time, you would say, 'Rwy'n mynd allan am bryd o bryd i'w gilydd'.

But don't be like Dafydd Nanmor. Go easy on the wine!

The warm stone walls of home beckon

It is said that an Englishman's home is his castle. The Welsh are often content with a cottage. The trouble is, such cottages have become so expensive. One of the reasons for this is the influx of settlers from over the border. They buy houses which could become first homes, so that they can have second ones, thence pushing up prices. There were almost 8000 second homes in the former Gwynedd alone in 1993. Well over 50% of homes in popular seaside villages can well be second ones. There are those who feel that the introduction of a property act could solve this problem, but others do not wish to tamper with a free market.

When we wish to differentiate between going home and being at home, we use two different words in Welsh, 'gartref' and 'adref'. Unfortunately, people often mix the two, but if you do so, you will be understood.

'Gartref' means 'at home' and 'adref' means 'homewards' and you could say, 'Fydda i ddim gartre(f) heddi(w)', or you might ask, 'Fyddi di gartre amser cinio?' These two examples do not show the expression of action.

On the other hand, you might say, 'Mae Huw wedi mynd adre i de', or you might ask, 'Ydy Alys wedi mynd adre'n gynnar?'

Note the expression of action here, Huw and Alys going home, not staying at home. If you wish to remark that Ceri is never home, you would say, 'Dyw Ceri byth gartre'.

Many speakers tend to forget that 'adre' exists and use 'gartre' all the time.

'There's no place like home', translates as, 'Does unman yn debyg i gartre'. There is also a well known proverb relating to home, 'Teg edrych tuag adre' (It is fair to look towards home). Note how the consonants t.g.d. at the beginning of the line are echoed or 'answered' in the second part. This is *cynghanedd*.

Putting boards on tables and decks

At one time you would find many titles in Wales that had the word 'Bwrdd' in them. 'Bwrdd Trydan' meant 'Electricity Board', 'Bwrdd Nwy' meant 'Gas Board' and 'Bwrdd Dŵr' meant 'Water Board'. The Welsh equivalent of the former Milk Marketing Board was 'Bwrdd Marchnata Llaeth'.

Many Welsh farmers regret the demise of the latter. When it was established in 1933, they were able to look forward, for the first time in their lives, to a monthly cheque for selling their milk to such a board.

But whilst south Wales farmers used to sell 'llaeth' (milk), North Wales farmers would sell 'llefrith' (again, milk), but ask for 'llaeth' in a north Wales Milk Bar and the waitress could well bring you a glass of buttermilk, referred to as 'llaeth enwyn' in south Wales.

The jugged milk is placed during teatimes on the 'board' or table. In Welsh, some people refer to table as 'bwrdd', but others refer to it as 'bord'. These two words know no boundaries, so be prepared for them. They both mean the same thing, but those who use 'bord' feel that 'bwrdd' should refer to other objects such as school chalk boards.

But further confusion might well arise as both words are not of the same gender, 'bwrdd' being masculine and 'bord' feminine. If you are invited to a meal in certain homes, you might hear, 'Dewch at y bwrdd', with no mutation after the article, but in other homes you might hear, 'Dewch at y ford', with the soft mutation after the article. King Arthur had his knights of the round table—in Welsh 'Marchogion y Ford Gron'.

The word 'bwrdd' is also used to describe the deck of a ship. 'Mae'r capten ar y bwrdd', means 'The captain is on deck' and by now you could well be forgiven for hoping that one of the meanings could be thrown overboard, or 'dros y bwrdd'.

Let the dancing commence! Summer is here!

The first of May used to be a time of festivity in Wales. According to the Celtic mode of reckoning this was the beginning of summer and the first of May would often be referred to as Calan Haf (the Summer Calend).

Many people practised transhumance. Around the first of May they would leave their winter abode (yr hendre) with their animals and move to their summer abode (yr hafod) and summer pastures. 'Hendre' and 'hafod' are used often in the names of town houses as well as farmsteads. The summer birch (y fedwen haf) would be erected, painted and be ribboned and young people would dance around it. This was called 'dawnsio haf'.

There are two words in Welsh that are used to express beginning. They are 'dechrau' and 'cychwyn'. To be strictly correct there is a shade of difference in the meanings of the two words. 'Cychwyn' is usually used when there is an expression of movement in a sentence. We might say, 'Mae'r car yn gwrthod cychwyn', or 'Dw i'n methu cychwyn y car y bore 'ma'. Here, 'cychwyn' is a verb noun (or the name of the verb). Used as a verb we might say, 'Fe gychwynnais i'r bore 'ma am wyth o'r gloch', or we might ask, 'Gychwynnest ti'n ddigon cynnar?'

To proceed to 'dechrau', you might say, 'Rown i'n dechrau cael llond bol ar y lecsiwn', or, 'Rwy'n dechre ca'l blas ar wersi Cymraeg'. A school pupil might ask her friend, 'Wyt ti wedi dechre dy waith cartre?'

You will often see on posters, 'Mae'r cyngerdd yn dechrau am saith'. A popular hymn concert on S4C is entitled, 'Dechrau Canu, Dechrau Canmol'.

Using both words together we might say, 'Dyw pobol yr Hendre ddim wedi dechre 'to; maen nhw'n methu cychwyn y car'.

But nostalgically, many young people would like to say, 'Bydd y dawnsio o gwmpas y fedwen haf yn yr Hafod yn dechre heno'.

Better late than never

Welsh-language magazines have a hard time in Wales in modern times because of low circulation figures. A few years ago, *Y Faner* ceased to exist. The first issue was published as a weekly newspaper in 1859 and it is said that at one time it enjoyed a circulation of 50,000. It had a strong and influential political voice and most of the people of Wales read the latest news on its pages. In 1977, with assistance from the Welsh Arts Council, it assumed a magazine format and had a circulation at that time of around 4,000. There is little hope that it will be revived. Despite the popularity of newspapers, most people nowadays hear the latest news on television.

'Diwethaf' (last, latest) and 'olaf' (last) are two interesting words in the Welsh language. Both can mean 'last' but 'diwethaf' (as well as 'diweddaraf') can mean 'latest'.

There is something definitive about 'olaf', for example, 'Ddoe oedd y tro olaf i fi fynd i'r dafarn yna'. This implies that I have no intention of going there again; but if you say, 'Neithiwr oedd y tro diwethaf i fi fynd i'r capel yna', I can assume that you might well go again next Sunday.

'Fe welais i e'r wythnos dwetha (diwethaf)', means that I saw him last week, but if you say, 'Dw i wedi'i gweld hi am y tro ola', I can assume that the lady in question has most probably died. Whatever has happened to her, you do not expect to see her again.

'Ymddangosodd y rhifyn olaf o'r *Faner* y mis diwethaf', would mean, 'The last issue of *Y Faner* appeared last month', but that particular month (not the defunct magazine) will be around again next year. What goes round comes round.

Jailed Joan's knightly affair

There is a stone coffin in Beaumaris church in Anglesey. It was dug up by a farmer in one of his fields and because of its useful shape he decided to use it as a pig trough. It was later realised that it belonged to Joan (or Joanna), the illegitimate daughter of King John of Magna Carta fame. She had undergone an arranged marriage with Llywelyn, the owner of the famous dog, Gelert. Its fictional grave (but not its remains) may be visited in Beddgelert.

Romantic tradition tells us that because of her confessed adultery with a Norman knight, William de Breos of Brecon, Llywelyn imprisoned Joan. She thought that he didn't love her, but because this was not so, he released her after twelve months. She died when she was still young.

Many becauses, and in Welsh we have a surfeit of prepositions for 'because'. Three are 'canys', 'oherwydd' and 'oblegid'. 'Canys' and 'oblegid' are still in use, but they have a biblical flavour and are not often used in everyday conversation. You can safely avoid them.

Adverbial clauses of reason are sometimes preceded by the preposition 'oherwydd', for example, 'Rhaid imi redeg oherwydd fy mod i'n hwyr'. 'Oherwydd' does not cause mutation, for example, 'Oherwydd cyfarfod arall, fedra i ddim dod'.

But a more commonly used preposition is 'o achos'. We might say, 'Rwy'n dysgu Cymraeg o achos rwy'n hoffi'r iaith', but in conversation, you will find that many speakers drop the 'o' before 'achos'. They might say, 'Mae yn y gwely achos 'i fod e'n sâl'. Strictly speaking this is incorrect. 'Achos' by itself means 'cause' and 'o achos' means 'because'. We would say, 'Y ci oedd achos y ddamwain o achos roedd e'n croesi'r ffordd ar y pryd', or 'Ces ddamwen o achos y ci'.

Note that 'achos' is also the Welsh for a court case and you could hear, 'Fe fydd yr achos yn Neuadd y Sir dydd Iau'.

In written Welsh, 'o achos' is usually adhered to and it is well to be familiar with the two meanings because you could be misunderstood; Llywelyn was.

Let's have a bit of sun and a primrose

According to tradition, the National Eisteddfod of Wales should be proclaimed by the Gorsedd at least a year and a day before the event. The ceremony is led by the archdruid, resplendent in his cream and white robes; all the other members will be wearing white, blue or green robes. The colours 'blue' and 'green' were introduced long after the Gorsedd became established. In other words, there have been changes over the years, but one wish that does not change is for the Gorsedd to be held 'yn wyneb haul, llygad goleuni' (in the face of the sun, the eye of light).

People may wear white robes either by invitation or by winning one of the chief eisteddfod awards; the blue robes may be worn only after passing an examination, and green robes are worn either by invitation or after passing an examination.

Two of these particular colours, together with 'yellow' can present problems to the learner because they (and they only) have both masculine and feminine forms. We could say, 'Mae car gwyn a gwisg wen gan yr archdderwydd'. Furthermore, we could say, 'Mae'r bardd yn gwisgo crys gwyrdd a gwisg werdd'. The Gorsedd's wish for a yellow sun to shine on the ceremony is not always realised, but it would be nicely symbolic also to have a yellow primrose (briallen felen).

When these colours are expressed singularly in the feminine form they take the soft mutation, 'gwisg wen' (not 'gwisg gwen'), 'gwisg werdd' (not 'gwisg gwerdd') and 'briallen felen' (not 'briallen melen'). These colours are always written (or expressed) in a mutated form; but when the nouns that they describe are in the plural, they become masculine. You would say 'gwisgoedd gwyn' or 'gwisgoedd gwyrdd' or 'briallu gwyrdd'.

Over the years the Gorsedd ceremony has been held in every county in Wales, but the first ever, a very simple affair was held on Primrose Hill (Bryn y Briallu) in London. That is why a primrose or two around this time would also be symbolic.

Gorsedd y Beirdd

Having a reverential peep at magazines

The first weekly news magazine, titled *Seren Gomer*, was issued in Wales in 1814. It was the brainchild of Joseph Harris who called himself Gomer. It contained foreign and national news, information about fairs and markets, movements of ships, letters and a poetry column. Due to a dearth of advertisements plus a crippling government tax, it had to cease publication after 85 issues.

Very few magazines are published today and those that are depend upon financial assistance from official bodies to make ends meet. One weekly magazine which depends on such assistance is *Golwg*. It has articles geared to those learning Welsh, but as yet has no column about the movement of ships.

Golwg is an interesting title for it, as the word itself has to work hard in the Welsh language. Basically, it means, sight, vision, but it can also mean view, look, or even admiration.

If a person has been blinded, we might say, 'Mae wedi colli'i olwg'. It is used also if you wish to know how a person might act under certain conditions. For example, you might say to a friend, 'Gyda golwg ar y farchnad, wyt ti am brynu'r tŷ?' Or again, 'Ar yr olwg gyntaf, mae'n dda'.

If a girl is inclined to day-dream, you might say, 'Mae golwg bell yn ei llygaid'. You would also use the word when referring to a person's sartorial habits. You could say: 'Dwy i ddim yn hoffi golwg yr hen ddyn yna', or 'I bob golwg, mae'n dda'.

If you want someone to cast a glance over your work, you might ask, 'Wnei di fwrw golwg dros hwn?' Again, if a grandfather dotes on a grandson, we might say of him, 'Mae ganddo dipyn o olwg o'i ŵyr'.

The plural form is also much used. If we wish to say that a person is looking up, we can say, 'Mae e'n codi'i olygon'. Put 'rhag' in front of the plural form and you have 'prospects' and can ask, 'Beth yw rhagolygon y tywydd heddi?'

Finally, if you think nothing of this article, you can say, 'Sgen i ddim golwg ohoni'.

I wish to be an English man

It is very unrealistic to quote the influx of English as the only reason for the demise of Welsh. The Welsh people themselves were often guilty of deliberately changing the language of the home. A very interesting example of this may be found in the biography of Thomas Jones, Rhymney. He became a very influential politician during the First World War and was a cabinet secretary to Lloyd George, the prime minister. When he was a child, Welsh was his home language, but as he progressed to secondary school, his parents decided not to speak Welsh at home, in the belief that English was the only language of progress. They thought that hearing English on the hearth would help their child. I quote this very sad tale merely as an example. There were very many other instances.

'Iawn' is a word that is often used in Welsh. It has more than one meaning. If you look a bit peaky, you might be asked, 'Wyt ti'n iawn?' On the other hand, if you answer a question incorrectly you could be told, 'Dwyt ti ddim yn iawn'. If you ask someone if he would like a cup of tea, he might answer in the affirmative, 'Iawn', but he would never say, 'Dim iawn'.

If you feel that something is good, you would say, 'Mae e'n dda'. If you feel that it is very good, you might say, 'Mae e'n dda iawn'. But many Welsh speakers are not happy with this simple, singular qualification, and might say, 'Mae e'n dda iawn, iawn, iawn'.

People often say, 'Diolch yn fawr iawn', but remember that 'iawn' here must follow an adjective. It is incorrect to say, 'Diolch yn iawn'.

Paying compensation in Welsh would be 'talu iawn'. Under old Welsh law, the father, grandfather, great grandfather, plus first, second and third cousins of a slanderer, as well as the slanderer himself, would have to pay 'iawn'—'Talu iawn am sarhad' (Paying compensation for slander). Welsh itself could well have a case here.

Small can be useful at times, dear

A few years ago, the smallest man in Britain lived in the Rhondda. His clothes had to be tailored for him and a selection may be seen in the Folk Museum at Sain Ffagan. If you would like to visit the smallest house in Britain, you need go no further than Conwy in north Wales. You will see the tiny terraced building, one up and one down, dwarfed by the towering castle nearby.

'Small' is an adjective that you will hear often in Welsh, but it is not always used to describe the size of an object. For example, you might hear someone asking a young child, 'Sut wyt ti, bach?' This would not be a reference to the child's stature; it would merely be a term of endearment. Similarly, someone might say, 'Mae hi wedi cael babi bach arall'. Baby would be quite normal in size—and loved. Were reference to be made to size, you could expect an additional remark such as, 'Ma fe'n un bach iawn'.

A child's story might well commence, 'Roedd hen ddyn bach a hen wraig fach yn byw mewn tŷ bach yn y coed'. It merely states that a dear man and a dear woman lived in a dear house in the forest. If you live in a tiny house, try not to say, 'Rwy'n byw mewn tŷ bach'. Some people might think that you live in a lavatory. 'Tŷ bach' is a term often used for 'toilet' in Welsh.

The adjective is sometimes used incorrectly. You might hear someone say (sometimes on the media), 'Bach iawn o amser sydd i fynd'. What is meant is, 'Ychydig iawn o amser sydd i fynd'. This mixing of 'bach' and 'ychydig' is becoming more common, so do not be confused.

A learner was caught in an endearing way once. She wished to emulate her tutor in all things, and (erroneously) accepted his eccentricity in naming his dog after a famous German composer. Not to be out-done, she decided to call her dog Handel as she had often heard her tutor saying to his Welsh corgi, 'Dere 'ma, bach!'

As you become hooked on Welsh, remember that 'bach' is Welsh for 'hook' also.

The hazard of crossing rivers

There has always been a close connection between Ireland and Wales, for example, the folk tales, The Mabinogion are familiar to most of us. They were translated into English in 1846 by an English lady, Charlotte Guest of Merthyr Tudful.

Most of the second of these tales is set in Ireland and describes an unfortunate marriage between Branwen and Matholwch, an Irish king. Her half brother, the giant, Bendigeidfran went to Ireland with his retinue to save Branwen from her misery and at one point he had to make himself into a bridge across the banks of a magic river. Whilst doing so he said, 'A fo ben bid bont' (Let he who would be a leader be a bridge).

Many Welsh people go to Ireland daily, but if they wish to tell you that they are doing so, they should not say, 'Rydw i'n mynd i'r Iwerddon'. The reason lies with the definite article, 'yr'. The rule in Welsh is simple; we use 'yr' before vowels, diphthongs and 'h'. We would say, 'Rwy'n hoffi eistedd yn yr haul', or, 'Cofiwch am yr iaith Gymraeg'.

But this rule can be quite pedantic when it comes to place-names. I noted on page 18 that we should not say 'Yr Iwerddon' or 'Yr America' or 'Yr Amwythig' or 'Yr India', but we can say 'Yr Almaen' and 'Yr Eidal'. You would sound ridiculous if you said, 'Rydw i'n mynd i'r Aberystwyth', but it is wise to say, 'Rydw i'n mynd i'r Wyddgrug'.

Bendigeidfran taught us to be wary of rivers. It is incorrect to say, 'Yr afon Rheidol sy'n mynd i'r môr yn Aberystwyth, nid yr afon Ystwyth'. The translation (with the definite article) is correct, but we do not use the article in front of the names of rivers in Welsh, so we say, 'Mae afon Hafren yn llifo trwy Lanidloes'. Purists are not happy if you say, 'Mae'r Teifi'n mynd i'r môr yn Aberteifi', dropping 'afon'.

But this is not true of all rivers that are familiar to us. A river that all Christians must cross one day is Jordan, and in Welsh we would say, 'Mae'n rhaid i bawb groesi'r Iorddonen', or, 'Mae afon yr Iorddonen ym Mhalestina'. Even Bendigeidfran could not have bridged this one.

Big can sometimes be very small

South Glamorgan was the smallest county in Wales but it could boast that it had, within its boundaries, three big constructions; for example, the biggest hospital in Wales is the University Hospital at Cardiff. It has more that 800 beds. It also has the biggest chimney, that of Aberthaw (Aberddawan) Power Station. If you want to get away from it all, you may do so from the biggest airport in Wales, but unfortunately the biggest aeroplanes cannot as yet land there.

When you think 'big' in Welsh, take care. The Welsh for 'big' is 'mawr' and you would say, 'Mae ysbyty mawr yng Nghaerdydd', but 'mawr' can be used to denote different kinds of 'bigness'.

If you are made a Presbyterian deacon, you may be required to sit in 'y sêt fawr' at the front. In reality, it is not big, but it seats big people; not because they are sizeably big but because society considers them to be important. We would say, 'Mae Dafydd yn ddyn mawr erbyn hyn'. That is, he has got on in the world.

We refer to the Christian God as 'Y Brenin Mawr' and when we wish to refer to a major road, we say 'y ffordd fawr' or 'yr heol fawr'. Here, we have the soft mutation as both 'ffordd' and 'heol' are feminine, but we could say, 'Does dim llwyth mawr ar y lorri fawr sydd ar y ffordd fawr', 'llwyth' (load) being masculine.

But in one negative sense, 'mawr' could also mean 'little'. You might hear someone say, 'Doedd gan y ferch fawr ddim amdani ar y traeth'. (Literally, the girl had hardly anything on her on the beach.) Here, 'fawr ddim' means 'hardly anything'. This occurs in negative forms and when 'fawr' refers to 'little' or 'not much', it is always mutated.

'Dyw punt fawr o werth erbyn hyn', means, 'A pound has hardly any value these days'. The word can also be useful in an ultra mild expletive that would not come amiss in 'y sêt fawr'. It is 'mawredd mawr' or 'big greatness'. A small word with a big job.

The blue green grass of home

Lingen, Symons and Vaughan Johnson were upper-middle-class Englishmen who lived in the nineteenth century. The three were all university scholars. In 1847 they published a report on the educational system in Wales, unfairly drawing attention to the inadequacy of Welsh education. One of their complaints was that monoglot children (and often teachers) could not speak English.

This report was published in blue books (see page 30) and became important symbolically as it incensed the public into action. It helped to foster a sense of nationality through outrage in the face of insult and the publication was referred to contemptuously as 'The Treachery of the Blue Books' (Brad y Llyfrau Gleision).

'Blue' has a variety of meanings in Welsh, the dominant one being the colour 'glas', but it can also mean green, grey, pale, silver, young and raw. We could say quite contentedly, 'Rwy'n gorwedd ar borfa las dan awyr las'. 'Gwelltglas' (literally, blue/green straw) is a word that we often use for 'grass' and we refer to green pasture as 'tir glas'.

We could also say, 'Mae gwallt y ferch yn glasu'. (The girl's hair is greying). The Welsh word for 'grey' is 'llwyd', but never say, 'Mae gwallt y fam yn llwydo', because in doing so you are implying that the mother's hair is becoming mouldy.

A mixture of milk and water is referred to as 'glastwr' (blue + water, the initial 'd' in this instance having hardened to 't') and if we wish to say that we have toned something down we use rather a big word, 'glastwreiddio'; for example, 'Mae wedi glastwreiddio'r erthygl'. (article).

'Dim ond glaslanc yw Dafydd', means 'Dafydd is only a (raw) youth', and should he faint for any reason, we might say, 'Mae'i wyneb e'n dechrau glasu' (His face is turning pale). We also describe silver coins as 'arian gleision', and might say, 'Does dim arian gleision gen i, dim ond arian papur'.

If someone is doing his level best, we would say, 'Mae'n gwneud ei orau glas'. This once caused problems to a Welsh speaker who said to an English friend that he was doing his blue best.

A bridge too steep

The record for the most famous but least used bridge in Britain should go to the old bridge at Pontypridd. William Edwards built the first bridge there in 1746 but this did not last long. He had three further attempts before his bridge finally stood up. Even then, people found it difficult to use.

His first mistake was to make the sides of his bridge too heavy and, like London Bridge, it all fell down. His last mistake was to make the bridge roadway too steep. Horses found it difficult to haul loads up one side and exceedingly difficult to hold loads back on the other side. During periods of low water, it was easier for carriers to ford the river instead.

There are two Welsh words for 'mistake', but it is possible that they had different shades of meaning at one time. The first word, 'camgymeriad' means 'error', and your tutor might tell you, 'Rydych chi wedi g(w)neud camgymeriad', or he might commiserate with you and say, 'Mae'n anodd peidio â gneud camgymeriad'.

The other word that is used is 'camsyniad', and to many of us, this means misconception or an erroneous view; a misapprehension. For example, 'Camsyniad yw credu fod pont Pontypridd yn bont dda', or 'Roedd gen i gamsyniad ynghylch y cyngerdd neithiwr'.

Using both words we could say, 'O achos camsyniad ynghylch marchnerth, gwnaeth William Edwards gamgymeriad' (Because of a mistaken view regarding horsepower, William Edwards made a mistake.) 'March' is stallion and 'marchnerth' is the Welsh for 'horsepower'. Some people use 'celrym', 'cel' being a shortened form for 'ceffyl' and 'grym' (in a mutated form here) meaning force.

In everyday conversation, many people use 'camsyniad' for both 'mistake' and 'misconception' and this is quite acceptable. Others amongst us have gone one step further and have adopted the English word in a Welshified form—mistêc. This is a mistake, and like that bridge, should be avoided.

Pont William Edwards, Pontypridd

Three feathers and three attempts for a Welshman

The three ostrich feathers are one of the badges of the Prince of Wales. Tradition says that they were adopted by the Black Prince after the capture of John, King of Bohemia at the battle of Crecy in the fourteenth century.

Tradition maintains also that he would not have won had not the famous bowmen of Llantrisant in south Wales joined his army. These archers were so good that they could fire up to ten arrows a minute. The motto under the three ostrich crest is Ich Dien, which means 'Rydw i'n gwasanaethu' (I serve).

'Tri' can be a tricky number for those who wish to have everything just right. One problem is that it takes both the masculine and feminine forms. You might say, 'Canodd y tri bachgen dair cân yr un'.

But mutating can change the meaning of a statement, and there is a subtle difference between 'Y tri cyntaf' (no mutation) and 'Y tri chyntaf' (aspirant mutation). 'Y tri cyntaf' (where 'cyntaf' is an adjective) means 'the first three'. You might say, 'Mae'r tri cyntaf yn cael mynd i mewn am ddim'. 'Y tri chyntaf' (where 'cyntaf' is a noun) means 'the three first', and 'Nhw oedd y tri chyntaf' would mean, 'They were the three first'.

This has an element of treiglophobia in it. In everyday conversation, it is difficult to maintain the differentiation. If an adjective follows 'tair' it takes the soft mutation. Eisteddfod people might say, 'Mae tair dda'n cystadlu heddiw'. 'Tair' does not mutate after the article and you would say, 'Mae'r tair merch wedi canu'n dda', and not 'Mae'r dair ferch . . .' But if you wish to refer to the third girl, you would say, 'Mae'r drydedd ferch wedi ennill'. You will be familiar with the saying, 'Three tries for a Welshman'. The Welsh would be 'Tri chynnig i Gymro', not 'Tri cynnig . . .'

Going back to those three ostrich feathers, we would say, 'Tair pluen estrys', 'pluen' being feminine, but 'tri estrys', ostrich being masculine. Shooting three arrows a minute might well be simpler.

Brave Gorsedd members should see red

Gorsedd members look resplendent in their white, green and blue robes during the eisteddfod ceremonies. I have mentioned previously on page 46 that at one time they were only robed in white, the green and the blue being introduced as the ceremonies developed, but should not red have been chosen instead of blue?

Welsh archers often wore green and white robes in battle. Henry Tudor, king of England, used green and white as his livery with a red dragon painted on it. The dragon on his shield (tarian), had its upper part in light red. The lower part was in gold. Elizabeth's dragon was similarly bicoloured, but she used a darker red, the colour used today.

Owain Glyndŵr sometimes had a golden dragon on a white field and he sometimes had red dragons. It was a compliment for every warrior to be called a dragon by the Welsh poets.

'Every' in Welsh is 'pob', but the meaning of a sentence can alter subtly as this word is mutated, i.e., there is a slight difference of meaning between 'pob' and 'bob'. If you say, 'Dw i'n mynd i'r eisteddfod bob dydd', you imply that you are going to the eisteddfod every day, 'pob' here being mutated at the beginning of an adverbial expression. You could say also, 'Rwy'n gwisgo esgidiau bob dydd'. This means that you are wearing boots every day, but if you say, 'Rwy'n gwisgo esgidiau pob dydd heddiw', you are saying that you are wearing everyday boots (and not your best boots). On the other hand, you would say, 'Rwy'n gwisgo ffrog bob dydd heddiw' (mutating) the mutating depending upon the gender of the word that precedes it, i.e., 'crys pob dydd' (masculine) but 'cot bob dydd' (feminine). But speakers and writers often choose to mutate 'pob' in both instances.

A very useful (and often used) idiomatic expression is 'bob o'. You could say, 'Cafodd y merched bob o hufen iâ gen i' (literally—Each of the girls had an ice cream by me). 'Cafodd beirdd y gadair a'r goron bob o wisg wen', would be, 'The poets of the chair and crown had a white robe each', but it is better to avoid this form when writing.

Smoking is bad for you

The first lawful printing press in Wales was set up in Adpar, near Newcastle Emlyn in 1718. It was established by Isaac Carter, and his first publication was a pamphlet on the evils of tobacco. Its message fell on deaf ears and many of his contemporaries felt that inhaling tobacco fumes was an excellent cure for chest ailments like bronchitis. Tobacco was also smoked in clay pipes during a nineteenth-century cholera epidemic in the belief that the smoke offered protection. Today, more people are aware of the dangers of smoking, and signs banning the habit are common in many public places.

Devising names for things related to tobacco has been causing problems in Wales. The Welsh for 'tobacco' is 'tobaco', with a single 'c'. This is often shortened to 'baco', but Welsh purists at one time devised the name 'myglys' (smoking plants), for the 'evil weed'. But this word was not inhaled into the Welsh word stream. The Welsh for 'cigarette' is 'sigarét', but you have at least three choices for a plural form. Many use 'sigarennau' whilst others use 'sigareti' but many feel that it is useful to adopt the English method of adding an 's' for the plural and they say 'sigarets', accented as in English, the same as with 'tomatos' and 'bananas'.

There are many who still favour 'ysmygu' for 'smoking', and it is a commonly used literary form, but the most commonly used oral form is 'smocio'. A Welsh literary translation for 'No Smoking', therefore, would be 'Dim Ysmygu'.

A commonly used English form for prohibiting smoking is, 'Smoking is Prohibited'. This is often translated into Welsh as, 'Ni chaniateir ysmygu', quite a mouthful, and you will be aware that speakers are prone to take short cuts.

'Caniatâd' means 'permission' but the Welsh word for 'prohibit' is 'gwahardd', the accent being on the ultimate syllable. A more correct translation, therefore, would be 'Gwaherddir Ysmygu'. Both 'caniateir' and 'gwaherddir' are impersonal verb forms and often cause difficulties to Welsh speakers as well as learners. A compromise is indicated here and there is nothing against saying and printing, 'Dim smocio', or, if you wish, 'Dim smocio yma'.

Famous, but not in Wales

An internationally famous Welshman, Richard Price, was born in 1723 in Llangeinor, Glamorgan, but he is not widely known in Wales. He sided with the American rebels during the American War of Independence and published influential works on federal government.

Another publication, *Observations on Revisionary Payments* led to the development of current life insurance and pension schemes. A stone from near his home has been placed in the Walk of Fame in America, but he refused the offer of American citizenship. He was a close friend of the American presidents, Washington and Jefferson.

The Welsh language has no indefinite article to correspond to the English 'a', but the definite article has three forms, 'y', 'yr' and ''r'. 'Yr' is used before vowels and diphthongs. You would say, 'Fe welais yr awyren yn uchel yn yr awyr', or 'Roedd yr ŵy wedi cracio yn y sosban'. 'Yr' is also used before the consonant 'h' and you would say, 'Mae cwmwl dros yr haul'.

Use 'y' before every consonant and the consonantal 'w'. You would say, 'Fe welais y wennol dan y bondo (eaves)', or 'Does dim llaeth yn y botel'.

Use ''r' after a vowel or diphthong. You might say, 'Aeth o'r ffordd a dringo'r wal i'r fynwent'. You should say, 'Mae'r ferch yn cysgu', rather than 'Mae y ferch yn cysgu', as the article should not be separated from the word preceding it if it ends in a vowel or diphthong, but this does not mean that no vowel can ever follow another vowel or diphthong; it often does this, for example, 'Gwrando ar y radio', or, 'Fe ddywedodd y gallai ddod erbyn saith'.

Note that the definite article must be used before 'rhain' (these). You may refer to famous people and say, 'Mae'r rhain yn *Y Bywgraffiadur Cymreig hyd 1940*', not, 'Mae rhain yn . . .'

Finally, they can be brought together in one sentence, 'Aeth y bachgen a'r ferch i'r dafarn ger yr ysgol'.

Richard Price was offered the Freedom of London in 1776, when Cardiff was a mere village. Such is fame.

The feminine touch can be effective—if it is red

Wales was invaded by the French in February 1797. Fourteen hundred soldiers landed near Strumble Head in Pembrokeshire, but they surrendered unconditionally, it is said because of the wiles of one woman. Her name was Jemima Nicholas. When she saw the invading army, she rounded up her friends, clad in their red shawls, and marched them around the headland carrying mattocks and spades. The French thought that they were members of the British Army and took fright. Some went to drown their sorrows in a local hostelry.

There is a monument in Fishguard Church to: 'Jemima Nicholas, a tall, stout, masculine female', who captured a dozen Frenchmen singlehanded and marched them off to the Fishguard guard-house.

'Hi', the Welsh for 'her' usually operates as a pronoun. It can (for example) operate as an independent personal pronoun. You might say, 'Fe welodd y milwyr hi'n dod'.

If you wish to say that a lady sang well, you might say, 'Canodd yn dda'. There is no need for you to say 'Canodd hi'n dda', unless you wish to emphasise the pronoun, for example, 'Canodd hi'n dda ond canodd e'n wael'.

It can also operate as a dependent pronoun. You might ask, 'Wyt ti wedi ei gweld hi'n ddiweddar?' Here again, it might be dropped in conversation and you can say, 'Wyt ti wedi'i gweld yn ddiweddar?'

But 'hi' has to work in other fields as well. For example, when referring to the weather, you might comment to a friend, 'Mae hi'n bwrw glaw'n gas'. This might appear strange grammatically as 'tywydd' is masculine, but we always refer to the quality of the weather in the feminine, 'Mae hi'n braf', or 'Mae hi'n oer'.

If a person becomes very drunk, people would not say bluntly, 'Mae hi/e wedi meddwi', but rather, 'Mae hi/e wedi'i dal hi'. (Literally, He/She has caught her, but the idiom will not translate).

If you feel that nothing more should be said in a heated argument, you can say, 'Taw piau hi' (taw = silence).

Nothing (or anything) but your money

Wales has its own traditional highwayman—Twm Siôn Cati. Like Robin Hood, he took nothing from the poor, but he was full of tricks. He sometimes hid in a cave, near the source of the river Tywi in Carmarthenshire. One day he was riding an old nag, with nothing but clinking sea shells in his saddle bag. A highwayman on a fine horse stopped him on a hilly track to demand this bag. Twm pretended to be terrified and threw the bag into a dense thorn bush. Swearing, the highwayman dismounted to retrieve it and Twm promptly mounted the fine horse and rode away, leaving the thief with nothing but a bag of sea shells—and the nag.

At one time, 'dim' meant 'anything'. There is a proverb which says, 'Heb Dduw, heb ddim'. (Without God, without anything), but over the years it has been used extensively in negative sentences and has developed an additional meaning, 'nothing'. For example, 'Beth oedd yn y bag? Dim ond cregyn môr'.

But 'dim' is often used incorrectly. It is incorrect to say, 'Gwn fod dim arian yn y bag'. What you should say is, 'Gwn nad oes dim arian yn y bag'. Unfortunately, this incorrect form is gaining in popularity and is often used by competent Welsh speakers.

'Dim' is also used to describe the figure 'zero'. If you want to say that you gave a book to somebody for nothing, you would say, 'Fe roddais i'r llyfr iddo fe am ddim'. The Welsh for 'Nothing but the best' would be, 'Dim ond y gorau'.

Idiomatically, if you wish to say that something is just right, you would use, 'I'r dim'; for example, 'Mae'r carped yn ffitio i'r dim'.

You can use 'dim' in an expression when you wish to say that something is almost empty, 'y nesaf peth i ddim' (literally—the nearest thing to nothing), for example, 'Doedd y nesaf peth i ddim yn y bag'.

And nothing can be seen in Twm Siôn Cati's cave today, not even a shattered sea shell.

Thomas the Tank Engine's great grandfather

Everybody should know that the first locomotive in the world to haul a load on tracks carried ten tons of iron from Penydarren, Merthyr Tudful to Abercynon. This occurred in 1804, over 20 years before Stevenson's Stockton to Darlington *Rocket* service. The tracks for the Stockton-Darlington line were made in Ebbw Vale. The fact that the famous locomotive was built in the town is commemorated on a monument in a well hidden corner of Merthyr; a humble and insignificant tribute to a remarkable engineer who worked in Wales.

The Welsh word for 'that' is 'mai', but it can be easily (and often is) confused with 'mae' (is). 'That' is used for emphasis before a noun clause. For example, you might say, 'Rwy'n gwybod mai ym Merthyr y mae Penydarren', or, 'Rwy'n credu mai fory yw'r diwrnod mawr'.

A word which is used colloquially instead of 'mai' in parts of south Wales is 'taw'. You might say, 'Rwy'n cofio taw fory mae pen blwydd Dewi'.

In conversation, people tend to say 'mai nid' (or 'taw nid') in the negative structure, for example, 'Clywais mai/taw nid hi a enillodd'. This should be avoided when writing Welsh. Instead you should use 'nad'. An example of the correct structure would be, 'Clywais nad hi a enillodd'. Or, you might ask, 'Ych chi'n siŵr nad Dilys oedd yn y car?'

In conversation, people often use 'mai' (or 'taw') after 'os', for example, 'Os mai ar ddydd Sul mae'r gêm, fydda i ddim yno'.

When you are writing, avoid both 'os mai' and 'os taw'. Instead, you should write, 'Os ar ddydd Sul . . .' It would be a good idea to write to British Rail to say that Trevithick's feat should be commemorated in a more prominent position, especially as the same locomotive carried 70 passengers as well.

Cofeb Richard Trevithick ym Merthyr Tudful

Ask for a golden mile of blood money

A stretch of road outside Bridgend in Glamorgan is known as the golden mile (y filltir aur). Iestyn ap Gwrgant, a lord in Glamorgan, could not get on with Rhys ap Tewdwr (Rhys son of Tudor) of Dinefwr. He therefore enlisted the help of Robert Fitzhammon, the Norman lord of Cardiff Castle, promising him a bag of gold coins if he could get rid of Rhys for him. A medieval form of contract killing and the mercenary Norman was happy to oblige; he slew Rhys in battle.

A meeting place was arranged for Iestyn to hand him the gold, but as Robert did not trust the Welshman, he commanded him to set the coins down in a row along the roadside. They stretched for one 'golden' mile.

Before measures were standardised, it was usual to use parts of the body for rough measurements. The Welsh for the measure 'foot' is 'troedfedd' (troed + fedd, or as long as the average foot). The Welsh for 'inch' is 'modfedd', or as long as the upper part of the thumb.

All these terms are feminine and you would say, 'Mae'r gadair un fodfedd o'r drws', but many speakers tend to disregard the soft mutation here and they might say 'un modfedd' (or 'un milltir'). This should be avoided.

You might say also, 'Mae'r cortyn fodfedd yn hwy nag un droedfedd'. In this example, the 'un' before 'fodfedd' has been dropped, but it still operates. 'Dim ond troedfedd oedd rhwng y ddau gar', would be, 'There was only a foot between the two cars'.

A Welsh rough measurement which is not found in English is 'ewinfedd'. In conversation, the initial 'e' is dropped. You might hear a person who wishes to make the most of a story say, 'Dim ond winfedd oedd rhwng y ddau gar'. 'Ewinfedd' means the thickness of a fingernail and is about the same as a hair's breadth (trwch blewyn).

Rumour tells us that not all those gold coins were collected afterwards. People who picnic near the Golden Mile could well be within a foot (or even an inch or a hair's breadth) of a fortune.

Remains that hark back to uneasy times

Offa was a king of Mercia in the eighth century. During his reign, there was constant strife between him and the Welsh, so he built a dike which extended from Bristol to near Prestatyn, a distance of about 100 miles. His aim was to keep the Welsh out of Mercia and any Welshman who crossed this dike might have to forfeit a limb, or even his life. Over the years, Offa's Dike has been a malignant expression and the remains of it can be seen in many areas along the boundary of England and Wales. The Welsh name for Knighton in mid Wales is Tref-y-clawdd (the town of the dike).

The name for 'remains' is 'olion'. Stick to the plural form as the singular form, 'ôl', can have other meanings. You could say, 'Mae olion Clawdd Offa ger Tref-y-clawdd'.

But if someone tells you, 'Mae ôl traed yma', he means that there are footprints here. Here, 'ôl' means mark. 'Gadawodd ei ôl yn y gegin', means that he left his mark in the kitchen.

But 'ôl' can take us to other neighbouring areas as well. 'There is nothing here', would be, 'Does dim ar ôl yma'. Here, 'ar ôl' means 'remaining'.

But it can also mean 'after'. 'Rhedais ar ôl y car', would be 'I ran after the car'.

The Welsh for 'back' is 'cefn'. You could say, 'Mae cefn tost gen i'. The Welsh for the lower regions of the back (behind) is 'pen ôl'. Should you wish to say that the chair is behind the table, you would say, 'Mae'r gadair tu ôl i'r bwrdd'. You could also say, 'Mae'r gadair tu cefn i'r bwrdd', but this structure is not often used.

Be careful when thinking of 'back'. You could instruct someone to take something back to the shop. Here, you might say, 'Dos ag e'n ôl i'r siop', or, 'Cer' ag e'n ôl i'r siop'. In the second example, you would be saying, 'Walk back with it', as 'cer'' is the command 'cerdd' (walk) without the ultimate syllable. Today, it means 'go', even if it is by car.

Use your car to go to see Offa's Dike by Knighton, and climb over the remains that mark a very uneasy time in our history.

The crafty devil never goes away

Devil's Bridge (Pontarfynach—'A bridge over Mynach') in the mountains of north Cardiganshire is one of the beauty spots of Wales. There, you may see three bridges, one above the other, crossing the turbulent river Mynach (monk). There were four bridges at one time but the most interesting one has long since gone. It was erected by the devil to help an old woman cross to fetch her cow. As payment he asked for the first living creature that crossed it. But the wise old woman took a bone from her apron pocket and threw it across the bridge. Her dog chased after it and the devil went away in disgust.

If you wish to say 'going away' in Welsh the form that you adopt could well depend on where you live. In south Wales, you might say, for example, 'Mae e wedi mynd bant i Lundain'. If you wish to warn someone to keep off the metaphorical grass, you would say, 'Cadw bant' (Keep away).

But in north Wales, the expression 'bant' is hardly ever used. There, they might say, 'Mae hi wedi mynd ffwrdd i Canada', or 'Cadw draw'.

'Pant' means 'hollow' and there is a proverb which states, 'I'r pant y rhed y dŵr' (Water runs into hollows—or, It is the people who have that receive).

The word 'mynydd' has experienced an extra, different meaning over the years, and is often used. The word 'mynydd' still means 'mountain', but the final consonant 'dd' was dropped and a new word, 'fyny' was created. You might say, 'Rwy'n mynd i fyny(dd) i Bontarfynach'.

If you invite friends to go with you as a group, you might say, happily, 'Bant â ni' (Away we go). But take care if you do, for when the devil went away he did say, 'I'll be back'.

A ravishing question of justice

The most notorious British judge of all times was born in Wales, in Acton Park between Wrexham and Chester. His name was George Jeffreys and it is said that the people of south-west England (where he dispensed 'justice') still think of him as 'Bloody George Jeffreys'. Even though he died three centuries ago, his name is still remembered with disgust. He judged 1,381 people guilty of high treason, he sentenced over 200 people to death and ordered the transportation of many hundreds to America and the Carribean. He sentenced many to be whipped and to rot and die in prison. It was rare for someone to get off with a simple fine.

The Welsh word for 'to fine' is 'dirwyo', but many people find the diphthong 'wy' quite difficult to say and there is a tendency for many to say 'dirywio' instead. For example, you might say wrongly, 'Cafodd y ficer ei ddirywio am yrru'n rhy gyflym'.

What you wish to say is, 'The vicar was fined for speeding', but 'dirywio' means 'degenerate', so be careful when you enunciate 'dirwyo', and remember, 'wy' and not 'yw'.

In the world of justice, the words 'trais' and 'treisio' can also cause some confusion in Welsh. 'Trais' means 'oppression', 'violence', and Cymdeithas yr Iaith often describes its activities as 'gweithredu di-drais' (non-violent action). 'Trais' is also used to describe a sexual attack. You might say, 'Cafodd y ferch ei threisio neithiwr'.

In order to avoid using 'treisio' people involved with the law sought a few years ago to invoke the assistance of another Welsh word that had been used to describe a sexual attack, 'rheibio'. Unfortunately, this word is used to describe 'to bewitch' as well as 'to ravish', and if a person says, 'Mae rhywun wedi rheibio'r ferch ger y castell', many a Welsh speaker might think that there was a witch around.

At one time, people did feel that certain country characters could cast spells (rheibio) and they were as feared as Judge Jeffries was, but the word 'rheibio' can be used in other contexts. For example, if your car won't start, you might say wryly, 'Mae rhywun wedi rheibio'r car yma'.

Sailing between two continents

Joseph Parry was described as the 'Supreme Composer of America' in his day, but he was born in Merthyr Tudful. He left Wales for Pennsylvania when he was fourteen years old but came back to Britain later to study at the Royal Academy of Music. He then returned to America. He was later appointed Head of Music at Aberystwyth College, and between his teaching commitments, his popular choir and his composing he was a very busy man. He crossed the ocean between America and Wales many times. He ended his career as a lecturer in Music at Cardiff, and is buried in Penarth. He composed over 400 hymn tunes, including the popular *Aberystwyth*. Most male choirs have *Myfanwy* in their repertoire. He composed the melody but nobody is certain who composed the words.

The Welsh for the preposition 'between' is 'rhwng'. It can be quite awkward to enunciate as it begins and ends with double lettered consonants that require some tonguing dexterity.

The good news is that there are no mutations after it, nor is the word itself mutated. The bad news is that it conjugates. You might say, 'Mae'r siop rhwng y capel a'r garej', and, 'Mae troedffordd (footpath) rhyngddyn nhw'.

It is used often when a person wishes to divulge an opinion in a secretive manner. You could say, 'Rhyngoch chi a fi, does dim arian ganddo fe'. It can also be used to express 'between' in a wider sense. You could tell children, 'Rhannwch yr arian rhyngoch chi', or 'Rhwng popeth, mae'n ddrwg yma'. Or again, 'Rwy'n methu penderfynu rhwng y ffrog goch a'r un las'.

Again, if you do not wish to be involved in an argument with two families, you might say, 'Rhyngddyn nhw a'i gilydd', which roughly means 'Let them get on with it'. The literary form for 'between them' would be 'rhyngddynt hwy', but the spoken form is 'rhyngddyn nhw'. There is no shorter form.

It is just as well to know what I could say should I wish you to solve your own problems, 'Nawr, rhyngoch chi a'ch cawl!'

If it's cheap, pay nothing, quickly!

Around a hundred years ago, one of the biggest stores in the world was situated in Wales. I refer to the Pryce Jones Establishment in Newtown, mid Wales. At that time, it sold most of its wares in response to mail orders and goods were dispatched to the four corners of the Earth. It could count world leaders amongst its customers. That type of store was new at that time and gained in popularity over the years because it could provide good quality commodities comparatively cheaply.

The Welsh word for 'cheap' is 'rhad', but it can also mean 'for nothing'. You might well see a service advertised in Welsh as being 'Yn Rhad ac Am Ddim'. Simply, it means 'free of charge' and a literal translation would be 'free and for nothing'. The repetition is unnecessary. They could say either 'Yn rhad' or 'Am ddim', but the expression has developed an idiomatic flavour over the years.

Someone might advertise an event in the local paper and use the phrase, 'Mynediad Rhad'. This means 'Free Admission', but on the other hand, you could well hear, 'Roedd dillad siop Pryce Jones yn rhad iawn'. This means, that the clothes were cheap. Without the qualifying 'iawn' you could not be blamed for thinking (or hoping) that they did not cost anything.

In situations such as these, use your common sense. If you are not in a situation where you could be led to expect something gratis, consider that 'rhad' means 'cheap'.

The Welsh version of 'Easy comes, easy goes', is 'A geir yn rhad a gerdd yn rhwydd' (What is obtained cheaply/free 'walks' easily). In this particular example, you have still another word that has more than one meaning. The second example 'rhwydd' here means 'easy/easily' but it can also mean expeditiously or quickly in certain parts of Wales. They could say, 'Mae'r car yn mynd yn rhwydd iawn'. The same could be said for money. 'Rhad' in either meaning is not commonly used in shops today.

The art of being straight despite the cold

Before the days of the tractor, ploughing matches were very popular amongst the farming community, much more popular than they are nowadays. A field would be divided into strips; each competitor would be required to plough this strip, using one or two horses and a single-share plough (aradr). The art was to plough (aredig) a straight furrow (cwys syth), each furrow resting tidily on the other. In the days of the tractor, speed is the essence, ploughs have three or more shares and a straight furrow is not deemed important. Hedging competitions would be held concurrently. The art here was to have straight stakes set at the correct angle (not vertical), in the ground, but the styles varied in different parts of the country. These competitions were usually held during winter months, the competitors shivering (sythu) in the cold.

The Welsh for 'straight' is 'syth', but it can have more than one meaning. In a ploughing competition, an adjudicator might say, 'Dydy'r gwys yna ddim yn syth'. But you could hear someone say, 'Mi es i adre'n syth ar ôl y gystadleuaeth'. He implies that he went home in a straight line and did not dawdle.

The verb noun is 'sythu'. You might say, 'Mae'n rhaid sythu'r gwys yna ar unwaith'. But remember that 'sythu' is used also to describe shivering with cold. A farmer might say, 'Rown i bron sythu wrth aredig y bore 'ma'.

If you wish to say that a fence post is set vertically in the ground, you would say, 'Mae'r polyn/postyn yn syth'. You could also say, 'Mae'r polyn/postyn yn unionsyth' (Union meaning direct, straight). Both words have a similar meaning in this context.

'Syth' can also mean 'as soon as'. You could say, 'Yn syth y gwelais i e, fe wyddwn fod rhywbeth yn bod'.

Hedging competitions are now enjoying a mini-revival. If you hear of one in your locality go straight there to see straight stakes set on tidy banks. You might well see 'tir âr' (ploughed land) nearby.

Ceffylau mewn cystadleuaeth aredig y tir

A whispered word carries far

The microphone was invented by a Welshman, David Hughes. He is thought to have been born near Corwen, but his family emigrated to the United States when he was seven years old. He presented his crude invention to the world in 1878. To the average person, it did not amount to much, merely a pile of rather rusty looking screws and wires, but with it he could make an audience hear a person whisper. Nobody thought at the time that it would cause such a revolution in broadcasting the spoken word.

'Siarad' is one of the first words that a learner commits to memory but what follows can sometimes cause problems. When you wish to say that you are talking to a person, beware of the English 'to' and do not think of 'i'.

It is wrong to say, 'Rown i'n siarad i Mam neithiwr', as a translation of 'I was talking to Mother last night'. The correct expression is, 'Rown i'n siarad â Mam neithiwr'. It is also wrong to say, 'Rwy'n mynd i siarad iddo fe'. Instead, you should say, 'Rwy'n mynd i siarad ag e'. Avoid also, 'Rwy'n mynd i siarad gydag e', as this could imply that both of you are going to address a public meeting.

'Siarad' is used in a few useful idioms; for example, if you wish to say that someone does not talk much sense, you would say, 'Dim ond siarad gwag ydy e'. Similarly, if you wish to talk about your work with somebody and you are asked what you are doing you would say, 'Rydyn ni'n siarad siop' (shop talk).

The letter combination 'si' is often pronounced 'sh', so 'siarad' is enunciated as 'sharad'.

In some parts of south Wales people say 'wilia' and not 'siarad'. 'Wilia' derives from 'chwedleua' or 'telling tales', 'chwedl' being the Welsh for 'tale' or 'fable'. 'Buon ni'n wilia trwy'r nos', would be, 'We talked all night'.

Incidentally David Hughes spoke of radio waves long before the German Hertz experimented with them, but scientists said of him, 'Mae'n siarad trwy'i het'.

No peace for the hero

Ellis Evans, a shepherd poet from Trawsfynydd, was killed on the battlefield in 1917. He had just submitted an ode on the subject 'Yr Arwr' (The Hero) to the chair competition at the National Eisteddfod which was held that year in Birkenhead. This was declared the winner and his *nom de plume* was called three times from the eisteddfod stage. It was then announced that he had been killed in action and a black cloth was draped over the chair. It is now know as Cadair Ddu Birkenhead.

A film based on his final years was shown on S4C. Before the third part (y drydedd ran) was shown, the phrase, 'Y Drydedd Rhan' was flashed on the screen. In this instance, the titler had omitted to mutate 'rhan'.

In mutation situations, the initial 'rh' and 'll' of certain words are often excepted, thus causing more treiglophobia. For example, you might say, 'Fe welais i'r ddrama neithiwr', 'drama' (feminine) being mutated after the article, ''r'. 'Llong' is also feminine, but you would say, 'Welais i mo'r llong ar y teledu' (no mutation) or, 'Fe brynais i'r rhaw (feminine) yn y ganolfan arddio'.

The two consonants do not mutate after 'un'. You would say, 'Un geiniog', or 'Un droed', both feminine nouns in their mutated forms, but you must say 'un llaw', or 'un rheol'.

An adjective following 'yn' (sometimes ''n') in the predicate can also be tricky. For example, you might ask, 'Ydy'r te'n boeth?' or 'Ydy'r dyn yn dal?' but, you must say, 'Dydy'r jwg ddim yn llawn', or, 'Mae'r tarw'n rhydd'.

After the pronoun 'ei' (his/her), correct mutation is crucial as it can alter the meaning. For example, 'Mae ei rhuban yn ei law', means that 'Her ribbon is in his hand'.

Ellis Evans' bardic name was 'Hedd Wyn', 'hedd' meaning 'peace'. The question, 'A oes heddwch?' could not be asked at this eisteddfod. The poet-hero was dead.

Keeping a welcome down the years

The first travel book that describes Wales was written in Latin in the twelfth century. Its author was Giraldus Cambrensis or Gerallt Gymro. In 1188 he went with Archbishop Baldwin on a recruiting campaign around Wales. They hoped to attract young men to go to liberate Jerusalem on the third crusade. One of the outcomes of this journey was the book, *Itinerarium Cambriae*. It is a book that is available in a Welsh translation and offers many interesting (albeit exaggerated) descriptions of how our forebears lived.

'Sydd' (or 'sy') is a much used word in Welsh. It means: 'who is, who are, which is, which are'. It is a combination of a relative pronoun and verb. It must not be confused with another word which is pronounced the same but is spelt differently, 'sudd' (juice). In response to your request for orange juice, you could be informed, 'Dim ond sudd afal sydd gen i'.

Quite often, as noted above, both in oral and literary forms, the ultimate syllable is dropped, and you might ask, 'Pwy sy'n dod i'r dosbarth nos Wener?'

As 'sydd' is a relative form, you cannot put a relative pronoun before it. It is incorrect to say, 'Mae'r dyn a sydd yn y car yn sâl'.

You should not be able to find 'sydd/sy'n' in negative clauses. You cannot say, 'Rwy'n gwybod am rai nag sy'n hoffi pysgod'. You should say, 'Rwy'n gwybod am rai nad ydyn nhw'n hoffi pysgod'.

On the other hand, you might well hear people say, 'Rwy'n gwybod am lawer sy ddim yn hoffi bwyta cig'. You will not find this structure in the grammar books, but it is acceptable in spoken forms, though 'nad ydyn nhw'n hoffi bwyta . . .' is the correct form.

Note that 'pwy' or 'beth' are often followed by 'sydd'. You might ask, 'Pwy sy(dd) yn y car?' or 'Beth sy(dd) yn y badell?' If a sentence begins with a noun instead of with a verb, again use 'sy(dd)'. You would say, 'Pysgod sy(dd) yn y badell'.

Gerald the Welshman often praised the Welsh for their hospitality. He could have said, 'Croeso cynnes sydd yng Nghymru'.

Where is the elusive Arthur?

King Arthur (if he ever existed) probably ruled over the Britons towards the end of the fifth century. The romantics among us like to dwell on his 'Welsh' origins; but the English are also eager to emphasise his 'English' roots and though nobody knows where he is buried, the most imaginative among us know that he has not died, that he went to Avalon Isle to recuperate from the wounds of battle, and is now asleep with his knights in a cave somewhere in Wales. We can ask, 'What cave?' or 'Which Arthur?' or 'How many warriors are sleeping with him?' or 'When did he live?' knowing full well that our questions will not be answered.

The Welsh for: 'what', 'which', 'how', 'when', is 'pa', but like King Arthur it is very elusive. I drew attention to it on page 20. There I warned you about an usurper, 'pwy' and I emphasised that 'pwy' is used when referring to persons. You may ask, 'Pwy oedd Arthur?' but you should not say, 'Pwy fedd sydd yng Nghlas-ar-Wy (Glastonbury)?'

'Pa' is often omitted in conversation. To be strictly correct, you could ask, 'Pa sawl marchog oedd gan Arthur?' but in conversation, what you hear is, '(Pa) Sawl wythnos sydd ar ôl?' Similarly, you could ask, 'Pa bryd mae'r cyfarfod?' but here again, the 'pa' is often dropped in conversation and you would hear, 'Pryd ma' te?'

You will be familiar with the word in a shortened form. You could ask, 'Pa le mae'r dosbarth?' but you would normally ask, 'Ble mae'r geiriadur?' Here, the initial 'p' is mutated and the 'a' dropped; but in literary forms 'pa le' is very much alive. Again, you could ask, 'Pa un sydd ore?' but you would probably say, 'P'un sydd ore?'

The initial 'p' can take all three mutations and you could stretch your imagination and sentencing capabilities and ask, 'I ba ynys aeth Arthur, ym mha le mae e nawr a pha bryd y daw e'n ôl?'

Tradition maintains that our Arthur will return one day to save Wales from its enemies. If he comes, he could probably capture this elusive 'pa' for us.

When spring comes, let's dance a carol

When Christmas comes upon us, many start planning a session of doorstep carol singing; to pay due respect to our Christmas traditions. But the word 'carol' has many meanings. Today we think of it as a religious Christmas song, referring mainly to the birth of Christ, but it was originally a dance to celebrate the shortest day in the calendar, and the knowledge that spring was near. The word was later used to describe a piece of poetry, composed to be sung to a familiar tune, and sung during many Christian festivals.

One of the Welsh words for 'many' is 'sawl', but like 'carol' it can have many meanings. For example, you might ask, 'Sawl un sy'n canu carolau heno?' or 'Sawl gwaith mae'n rhaid i fi ddweud wrthot ti?'

In these two examples it is used in an interrogative form, but to be strictly correct, you should be asking, 'Pa sawl . . .?' You will see this structure often in written forms but in conversation, as I noted on page 75, the initial 'pa' is often dropped.

But it can be used simply as a translation of 'many'. You might say, 'Mae sawl plentyn wedi bod yn canu carolau heno', but here you must beware. Bearing the English syntax in mind, many learners might wish to say, 'Mae sawl plant . . .' as a translation of 'Many children . . .' Think of 'Many a child' instead. If you see the word 'sawl' in a structure, use it as a clue and consider the singular.

But 'sawl' can, in certain instances, mean 'he' or 'she'. You could say, 'Mae'r sawl sy'n dawnsio carolau'n cadw traddodiad'.

So, if you wish to maintain a tradition next Christmas, go out to dance a carol or two.

A day to remember, perhaps

The first day of the year is described in Wales as Calan Ionawr. 'Calan' (Calend) may be considered as the first day of a new year, but the word may be used also to describe the first day of any month and 'Calan Mai' is a familiar expression.

For centuries up to 1752, the Church had been celebrating 'calan' on 25 March, but the Gwaun valley in Pembrokeshire still celebrates another 'calan' which is referred to as 'Hen Galan'. This occurs on 12 January. Many years ago the good people of Llandysul would celebrate the occasion with a soccer match which lasted all day and would have become quite heated before sunset.

The Welsh word for 'day' can be either 'dydd' or 'diwrnod' but the two words are not always interchangeable; for example, in a greeting situation, you might say, 'Dydd da ichi', but you will not hear people say, 'Diwrnod da ichi'. On the other hand you could say, 'Roedd calan slawer dydd yn ddiwrnod i'w gofio'. Here, you could also have said, '. . . yn ddydd i'w gofio'.

If you wish to refer to a day that will probably never come, you will say, 'Dydd Sul y pys', for example, referring to a lazy person you could say, 'Fe wnaiff ddiwrnod o waith ar ddydd Sul y pys'. Here, you would usually say, 'diwrnod o waith' and not 'dydd o waith'. But if you wish to spend a day doing nothing, a day of leisure, you would usually refer to it as 'diwrnod i'r brenin' and not 'dydd i'r brenin'.

If someone loses a fight (against death, for example), people would say, 'Mae e/hi wedi colli'r dydd' (literally, He/she has lost the day). This is a familiar idiom and people would not say, 'colli'r diwrnod'.

The day begins, of course, with the dawn, and when we say that dawn is breaking we say, 'Mae'n dyddio' (day-ing). On the first of January, you might start a new diary. The Welsh for 'diary' is 'dyddiadur' (dydd + iadur), where you record what happens every day.

Descriptions can give wrong impressions, even while ironing

Waldo Williams was one of our greatest poets. He was born in Haverfordwest (Hwlffordd) to an English-speaking mother and a Welsh-speaking father. When Waldo was seven, he moved with his family to Mynachlog-ddu, a village in the north of the county. He quickly mastered Welsh and fell in love with the language. He composed one of his best remembered poems, 'Y Tangnefeddwyr' when he was near his home one snowy night early in the last war and could see the sky above Swansea glowing rosily as German bombs destroyed the town centre. The first lines run: 'Uwch yr eira wybren ros/Lle mae Abertawe'n fflam' (Above the snow a rosy sky/Where Swansea is aflame). He ended each verse with the couplet, 'Gwyn eu byd, tu hwnt i glyw, Tangnefeddwyr, plant i Dduw' (Blessed are they, beyond hearing, peacemakers, children of God) a reference to his departed parents. He published one volume of poetry, *Dail Pren*. In an article in *The Western Mail* a few years ago, the title was incorrectly translated as 'wooden leaves'. Such an error is understandable if one thinks of English when translating.

'Dail pren' means 'the leaves of a tree'. Here, 'pren' does not operate as an adjective, (as in 'ceffyl pren'—wooden horse); furthermore, 'pren' can refer to both 'wood' and 'tree' in Welsh. You could say, 'Mae llawer o ddail ar y goeden' or 'Mae llawer o ddail ar y pren'.

It is unusual for the adjective to precede the noun in Welsh, but when it does, pay attention to how it operates. I have previously mentioned the subtle difference between 'hen ddyn' and 'dyn hen' (page 22); for example, 'cam farnu' means 'misjudging'. 'Cam' here means wrong. Cam-drin means abuse, in an expression such as 'cam-drin plant', but if we say 'pren cam' we mean that the piece of wood is crooked.

If we adhere to the English pattern, we can use adjectives inappropriately in Welsh. If you say, 'Ces sioc drydanol neithiwr', you should be saying that you had an electrifying shock last night, but if you say, 'Ces i sioc drydan wrth smwddio', you are saying that you had an electric shock whilst ironing, so beware of electricity—and adjectives.

Waldo Williams a'r gofeb iddo ym Mynachlog-ddu

If you want it, ask properly

The first monastery in Wales was built on Bardsey Isle (Ynys Enlli), about three kilometres beyond the tip of the Llŷn peninsula. Tradition maintains that twenty thousand saints are buried there. Monasteries were built on islands like Caldey (Ynys Bŷr) in Pembrokeshire and Puffin Island (Ynys Seiriol) in Anglesey as the monks wanted peace and quiet, but should you want to express a wish for peace and quiet in Wales, it might be well for you to pay attention to a grammatical detail. It is incorrect to say, 'Rydw i eisiau heddwch', or 'Rydw i eisiau dillad newydd'. The correct expression is, 'Mae arna i eisiau heddwch'. The grammar of the language states that 'ar' should always be used with 'eisiau', but as the non standard version is more flexible to the tongue it often supplants the grammatically correct version.

In north Wales, the expression has been contracted, and a book published a few years ago is titled, *Tisio tshipsan?* (Do you want a chip?) 'Tisio rhagor?' (Os arnat ti eisiau rhagor/Do you want more?) is often used in conversation.

You may safely follow the crowd in this respect as language is constantly in a state of flux but as the standard version is common in its written form you should be familiar with it.

One way of avoiding the expression is to use another word that is common in south Wales, 'ymofyn' but you would hardly ever hear anybody saying, 'Dwy'i ddim yn ymofyn trafferth'. It is probably not a word you would look for in a dictionary under the appropriate initial letter as you would not be aware of it. In conversation, the initial 'y' and the middle 'f' (mo'yn) have been eroded, and what you would hear would be, 'Wyt ti'n mo'yn (moyn) mynd i Ynys Enlli?' You can look in vain for 'mo'yn/mofyn' in most dictionaries but it is listed in *Geiriadur Gomer i'r Ifanc* (1994).

Similarly, on Ynys Enlli, you will look in vain for twenty thousand graves. If you wish to have a secluded holiday, you may rent a cottage there in summer, but bring your chips with you.

Waiting together for Britannia

Together, the Britannia and Telford bridges bear traffic to and from Anglesey. Rail travellers who use the Britannia bridge can see statues of two lions seated by the roadside. Together they guard the bridge and years ago they inspired a rustic rhymester to muse, 'Two lions fat, sitting down flat, one ochor this and one ochor that' (over here and over there). But why the name Britannia?

The original intention was to have the two lions together guarding a statue of Britannia above the bridge, but the cost of the bridgework had exceeded the financial estimates and Britannia had to be forgotten for the time being.

'Together' translates into Welsh as 'gyda'i gilydd'. You might say, 'Mae'r ddau lew yn gorwedd gyda'i gilydd wrth y bont'. But problems can occur in written forms. This sentence, for example, is grammatically defective: 'Maen nhw'n gweld eu gilydd bob dydd'. Here, 'eu' should have been written as 'ei'.

The Welsh for 'his', 'her', 'its' is 'ei' (the singular form) and for 'their' is 'eu' (a plural form). You would say, 'Mae ei merch yn sâl' or, wrongly, 'Maen nhw'n gweld eu gilydd yn yr ysgol heddiw'.

In the above example, 'eu gilydd' should have been written as 'ei gilydd', as it is a singular structure. It can appear to be a plural form as 'Maen nhw' translates as 'They are', but the word 'cilydd' (not mutated here) in 'ei gilydd' means 'companion', so, technically speaking, each one was with his (or her) companion, thus continuing a singular form. When writing therefore, never write 'eu gilydd'. It is always 'ei gilydd'.

In both spoken and written forms, the initial 'e' is dropped after a vowel and you have ''i gilydd'. For example, 'Mae'r ddwy bont gyda'i gilydd yn cynnal llawer o draffig'. But the two lions fat are still waiting for Britannia.

More trees, sheep and bent rules

There are many more sheep than people in Wales. There are many more trees in the former Glamorganshire than in any other county in England and Wales. There are still more in Scotland—Yr Alban. There are more Welsh speakers in the former Glamorganshire than in the former Gwynedd. The city/town with the most Welsh speakers is Swansea. There are more place-names in Wales beginning with the word 'Llan' than any other prefix.

Which brings me to the point that the two words for 'more' can sometimes cause confusion in Welsh as they are not always interchangeable. The comparative form of the adjective 'mawr' is 'mwy' and it means 'bigger'. We would say, 'Mae ŵy gwydd yn fwy nag ŵy iâr'. This is probably the more commonly used meaning.

'Mwy' can also mean 'more', and you may ask at table, 'Mwy o de, rhywun?' If you did not appreciate the welcome, you might vow never to visit the house again and say, 'Byth mwy!' Here, mwy means 'again'.

There is more. A word that can often be used instead of 'mwy' is 'rhagor'. Indeed, many a host would ask, 'Rhagor o de, rhywun?' The natural response could well be, 'Na, dim rhagor, diolch'. Purists might well not be happy saying, 'Na, dim mwy, diolch'.

Again, you cannot say, 'Mae car Dan yn rhagor na char Huw'. In this instance, 'rhagor' and 'mwy' cannot be interchanged to compare either eggs or cars, or anything else. 'Rhagor' cannot mean 'bigger', but it can mean 'better' after adding an 'i'; for example, you might say, 'Mae Dan yn rhagori ar Huw mewn mathemateg'.

Purists should never say, 'byth rhagor' instead of 'byth mwy'. Dictionaries do not include 'again' in their definitions of 'rhagor' but you could well hear this expression creeping into conversation as more and more rules are bent in conversation.

Observe the conditions and get it right

Had you been alive and living in Pontypridd on 23 January 1993, you would have been agog with the latest titbit of news; the death at ninety three of the eccentric father of Iesu Grist (Jesus Christ). He was known locally as Doctor William Price, the pioneer of cremation. He believed in free love, was a staunch vegetarian, and was a familiar sight in Pontypridd, walking around with a fox fur on his head. In 1884 he was accused of burning the body of his infant son, whom he had named Iesu Grist, but was found not guilty.

'Pe' (if) followed by a verb is a much used construction in Welsh. This particular verb is either in the imperfect tense of the subjunctive mood or in the pluperfect tense of the indicative mood. Some grammars refer to it as the conditional tense, as a person's response to a situation is conditional upon some other factor. For example, in conversation, you might say, 'Pe bawn i yn dy le di, fe fyddwn i'n mynd' or 'Pe bait ti wedi dod, fe allen ni fod wedi mynd gyda'n gilydd'. Or again, 'Pe bai e/hi'n gall, fe fydde fe/hi'n aros gartre'.

There are variations, for example, you could hear 'Pe tawn' instead of 'Pe bawn'. You might say, 'Pe tawn i'n well fe fyddwn i'n falch' or 'Pe tai'r car gen i, fe allen ni fynd'.

The negative form is quite simple; simply include 'na' after 'pe'. For example, you could say, 'Pe na bai'r car wedi torri, fe allen ni fynd'. Some people say, 'Pe bai'r car ddim wedi torri, fe fyddwn i mewn pryd', but this is not standard Welsh.

If you ever go to Llantrisant in Glamorgan, don't forget to go to see the monument to Dr Price at the Bullring, or 'Pe baech chi'n mynd i Lantrisant, ewch i weld y gofgolofn i Dr Price'.

Caught paying respects long since due

Evan Evans was the foremost Welsh classical scholar of the eighteenth century. He was brought up in Lledrod, Ceredigion, was educated locally, and progressed to study in Oxford University. He took holy orders but remained a curate all his life, mainly because of his intense interest in early Welsh poetry, a pastime frowned upon by the Church of England in Wales. He was amongst the first to draw attention to the richness of this early poetry and spent much of his time laboriously copying examples from manuscripts in various mansion houses. He was also a poet and was sometimes referred to as Ieuan Brydydd Hir (Ieuan the Long Poet).

Many centuries ago, it was common for someone who was tall to be described as being long. This word was superseded in this particular context by a word borrowed from the English, 'tal'. But the unwary can be easily caught by the word in various forms.

You might say of someone, 'Mae e'n dal iawn', but you could also say, 'Rydw i'n dal annwyd yn hawdd'.

It can be still more confusing if the 'a' is circumflexed, because then it means 'payment'. You could say, 'Ces bunt yn dâl am y llyfr'.

You might come across 'tal' prefixed to words referring to payment. Careful people write on their cheques, 'Cyfrif y talai yn unig' (The account of the payee only).

We are encouraged not to drink too much intoxicating liquor for obvious reasons, but if you wish to say that a person is drunk, you can offer a much used idiom, referred to on page 60, 'Mae e wed'i dal hi'.

Orally, people often add an 'a' to 'dal' when it means 'to catch'. You might hear a boastful fisherman say, ''Dw i 'di dala pysgodyn mawr'.

Evan Evans received hardly any pay for his years of toil. If you would like to pay a visit (talu ymweliad) to his grave in Lledrod cemetery, don't bother. Nobody knows where it is.

A time to stop—and start

In *Julius Caesar,* by Shakespeare, Cassius says, 'The clock has stricken three' but there were no clocks in Julius Caesar's time. However, there was a clock in Milan in 1335. Soon after, clocks were here in Wales. It is possible that a clock is first referred to in Britain in a poem written by Dafydd ap Gwilym who would have been a young gentleman poet living near Llanbadarn when the Milan clock was telling the time.

In this particular poem he complains that he was sleeping, dreaming that he was in bed with a comely girl when he was woken by a clock. The noise this clock made resembled a dog chewing a dish and he curses it for interrupting such a beautiful dream.

Here, I turn to the Welsh word for 'here'—'yma'. But 'yma' also means 'this'.

You will be familiar with, 'Tyrd yma' or 'Cer(dd) o 'ma' (Go from here or Come off it). A school child who is present in class responds with 'yma', to a teacher during registration. If you enter an empty room, you might say, 'Does neb yma'. You could also say, 'Mae'r stafell (y)ma'n wag', or 'Mae'r cloc 'ma wedi stopio'. Also, you might say, 'Rown i'n sâl y bore 'ma', or 'Fe fydda i yna'r pnawn yma'.

You might well hear someone say, 'Wyt ti'n dod heno 'ma?' or 'Wyt ti'n mynd (y)fory 'ma?' Such questions are grammatically incorrect. You can say 'This morning', 'This afternoon', or 'This night' in Welsh, but you should never say 'This tonight', or 'This tomorrow'.

It is easy to see how this has come to pass in spoken Welsh. A few speakers do not realise that whilst 'bore' and 'pnawn/prynhawn' are masculine nouns, 'heno' and 'yfory' are adverbs and are uneasy with an 'yma' appendage.

You will sometimes hear the erroneous expression on sound radio and television, but it is as intrusive as poor Dafydd ap Gwilym's clock.

A mixture of awkward sixes

The Church in Wales has a bench of six bishops, in Abertawe and Aberhonddu (Swansea and Brecon), Bangor, Llandaf, Llanelwy (St Asaph), Mynwy (Monmouth) and Tyddewi (St David's). Since it broke away from The Church of England in 1920, Wales has had its own archbishop. The first to be appointed was the Bishop of St Asaph. Since then all archbishops have also been bishops in one of these six dioceses, but some people have suggested that administratively it would be better for the archbishop to have his chair in Llandaff Cathedral. As a bishop's duties are heavy they feel that he should not be in charge of a diocese as well, i.e., one plus six and not one of six.

'Six' causes problems to many speakers. The rule is that the final 'ch' in 'chwech' is dropped before nouns and we have, 'Mae chwe esgob yng Nghymru', or, 'Fe welais i chwe merch yn y siop'. The spirant mutation always follows 'chwe', so we would say, 'Mae'r stamp yn costio chwe cheiniog', but there is a tendency to ignore this mutation in the spoken form and you might hear, 'Mae chwech castell yn y sir'.

A few grammar books might draw attention to a 'wrong' mutation here. Take birthdays, for example. Many people might say, 'Mae Gwen yn chwe mlwydd oed', and others might say, 'Mae Alun yn chwe blwydd oed'. Both expressions are old and quite acceptable. 'Mlwydd' is easier to slip off the tongue than 'blwydd'. So you can say, if it applies, 'Rydw i wedi bod yn siarad Cymraeg am chwe mlynedd'.

If you wish to avoid dropping the final 'ch' in expressions like 'Chwe esgob', you can introduce 'o' (of) into your sentence and say, 'Chwech o esgobion', or 'Chwech o ferched'. Should you wish to escape from these awkward Welsh sixes, do not venture into a toilet. Sometimes, this is referred to in north Wales as 'lle chwech'. This is not an allusion to a meeting place for six bishops as many toilets accommodated six people at one time.

Eglwys Gadeiriol Llandaf

Lie back to think of English beef

When people refer to the roast beef of old England, they should remember that this succulent fare originated in Wales. In the eighteenth century Wales was one of the chief cattle breeding areas in the British Isles. A familiar sight during the summer and early autumn months would be black cattle being herded over the Welsh mountains to be fattened on the richer pastures around London. The cattle dealers were often astute businessmen with a strong romantic streak, influenced by fashion. Before returning home they would often buy items of clothing for their wives, and a lady from a village like Tregaron in Ceredigion could well step out dressed in the latest Paris fashion.

Some English words influence Welsh more than others. A word that does a great deal of erosive harm is 'to'. I have mentioned previously (page 19) that people use expressions like, 'Rwy'n mynd i'r meddyg/deintydd', instead of 'Rwy'n mynd at y meddyg/deintydd', wrongly using the incorrect 'i' instead of 'at' for 'to'. It is common for people to cut corners in conversation but in the case of 'to', people will often include a translation of the preposition when it is unnecessary. The more correct version slips much more easily off the tongue.

It is correct to say, 'Rwy'n mynd i Lundain fory', but if you wish to say that you must go to London tomorrow, there is no need for you to say, 'Rhaid i fi (i) fynd i Lundain fory'.

I quote a few examples here with the superfluous prepositional 'i' in brackets: 'Mae'n bwysig i ni (i) ddod heno. Gofiwch chi (i) brynu llaeth? Ydy hi'n deg (i) (d)dweud nad yw'n ffasiynol? Mae'n hoffi (i) (f)mynd i'r dre i siopa. Rhaid cofio (i) (d)darllen hwn'. In all the above instances you may safely ignore the intrusive 'i'.

When the drovers were preparing to return to Wales they were careful to leave the language where it was. We now have it, so be careful when you think of 'to'.

Should Dewi join a little learners' class?

One of the most important days on the Welsh calendar is St David's Day. Different from the saints of England, Ireland and Scotland, David is the only person who was born in the country of his sanctification. George is a myth. Dewi died on 1 March, but the exact year of his death is unknown. Were he able to perform a miracle and return to Wales, he would not be able to make head nor tail of any of the two languages of this article. Nor would we be able to understand him if he offered us his famous advice in the Welsh of his day, 'Gwnewch y pethau bychain' (Do the little things).

'Bychain' has a plural form in that sentence and means 'bach'. 'Bach/bychan' are nearly always interchangeable. 'Bychan' also has a feminine form, 'bechan' which is mutated (fechan) in conversation. The plural has no feminine form. We would say, 'Bachgen bychan a merch fechan', but 'merched bychain'.

At one time it was ruled that a feminine adjective should follow a feminine noun. This rule has long since been ignored in most instances, but still operates in a few. I have already referred to masculine and feminine adjectives describing colours, (paent gwyn/torth wen; car gwyrdd/ffrog werdd—page 46) but there are other very common feminine forms which are always used, for example, you might say, 'Mae dadl gref ganddo fe'. You would not say, 'dadl gryf'. Furthermore, you might say, 'Rwy i am sgrifennu stori fer', and not 'stori fyr'. You would also say, 'Mae afon Hafren yn afon ddofn' (not 'ddwfn'). A very common place name is 'Ffynnon Wen'. If you said 'Ffynnon Gwyn', we would assume that you were referring to Gwyn's well.

Other masculine/feminine forms which are very common are: llym/lem (sharp); tlws/dlos (pretty); trwm/drom (heavy), llwm/lom (bare); crwn/gron (round). Note the vowel change in the feminine in all these examples.

At one time 'Fychan' was a popular surname. You could meet a man who would describe himself as Dafydd Fychan. Under the influence of English, people sought to Anglicise these forms and Fychan became Vaughan. Some might say, a little unwise thing to do.

Capture the king but watch how you go!

A form of chess was popular in Iran as early as the seventh century. The game had arrived in Wales by the eleventh century and was among the twenty four feats (pedair camp ar hugain) in the Middle Ages. There is reference to playing chess in the Mabinogion. King Arthur possessed gold chessmen and possibly liked a game after his evening meal. Before preparing to go to battle, warriors used to play 'gwyddbwyll' (chess) and old pieces may be found in museums, many intricately carved. Since 1970 Wales has had its own Chess Federation.

The Welsh for 'to go' (mynd) is an irregular verb that can cause problems. If you wish to say that you are going to the class every day, you might use the periphrastic form, '(Ry)dw i'n mynd i'r dosbarth bob dydd'. The shortened form of this third person singular verb would be, 'Af i'r dosbarth bob dydd'. This structure is not often used at the beginning of a sentence, but you could come across it in a sentence like, 'Â Huw i'r gwaith erbyn naw bob dydd' (Mae Huw'n mynd i'r gwaith erbyn naw bob dydd). Note that the 'â' ('goes') must be circumflexed.

But the shortened form is often used in a question pattern. While playing chess, you could ask, 'I ble'r af fi nawr?' or 'I ble'r a' i nawr?' The periphrastic form would be, 'I ble ry(dw) i'n mynd nawr?'

But there's a slight difference of meaning between the two expressions. In the first you could be asking for advice in a perplexed way. The second could be a simple query regarding direction.

In conversation, you probably would not say, 'Â'r plant i'r gwely cyn wyth bob nos'. Instead you would say, 'Aiff y plant i'r gwely . . .' or 'Mae'r plant yn mynd i'r gwely . . .'

'Aiff' (an oral construction) is rapidly superseding 'â' in conversation and is also creeping into children's books and dialogues in novels. You can also hear, 'Fe/Mi aiff . . .'

Think of chess, and ponder carefully before you go.

Don't drop your stitches

Years ago, the 'noson wau' (knitting evening) was a common feature of rural life. The hostess would prepare well before hand, baking various cakes and white bread. She would then invite young men and women with their knitting wool and needles; this being a way for them to get to know each other better. In addition to the chief task of knitting stockings, there was also an opportunity to catch up on the local gossip or to listen to the story-teller.

The Welsh word for knitting needle is 'gwaell', but it is not often used. However, the plural form (gweill) is used often by news-readers, despite the demise of the 'noson wau'. A (metaphorical) sentence that you could hear would be, 'Mae gan y cwmni lawer o bethe ar y gweill' (literally—'The company has many things on the knitting needle', though there is no knitting involved).

The first step in knitting a stocking would be the casting of stitches (pwythau) on to the knitting needles. If a person has plans he proposes to execute, he might say, 'Mae gen i gynllunie ar y gweill', though he has never cast a stitch.

If workers are made redundant, you might hear a person say, 'Mae cant o bobol ar y clwt nawr'. You could say, 'Mae Huw ar y clwt ar ôl colli'i arian'.

'Clwt' (clout) has many meanings. It could mean a piece of cloth, a chip of stone from a slate or a piece of land. In the above sentence, there is a suggestion that Huw is so poor that he has no more than a piece of land on which to rest his head. With reference to a piece of cloth, a well known idiom is, 'Gwell clwt na thwll', implying that repaired clothing is preferable to holed clothing.

News-readers sometimes say, 'Mae'r cyfan yn y fantol'. (Everything is in the balance), 'mantol' being the Welsh for 'balance', a word that is used mainly in this idiom. It is frequently used in the Welsh for balance sheet, 'mantolen'.

If the 'noson wau' story-teller could knit a good ghost story, the young women would welcome company on the way home. It was then up to the men not to drop any metaphorical stitches.

In a way, a chapel is a church, perhaps

The Latin for a small mantle is *capella*. From this came the Welsh word 'capel' (chapel). Initially the word was simply used to describe a small secluded place for worshipping. Many churches, mansion houses and schools have chapels within them. Today, the word 'chapel' is usually used to describe a box-shaped Nonconformist meeting place. These chapels have been described as 'blychau bychain Duw' (God's little boxes).

When we refer to a church, we might think of a building that usually faces east and has an altar. But over the years, chapelgoers have been using the word 'capel' to describe the building in which they worship and 'eglwys' to describe the society of people who worship in that building. They do not always adhere rigidly to this division and it can sometimes cause confusion.

You might hear a person say, 'Rwy'n aelod o eglwys Carmel', but he might go on to say, 'Rwy'n mynd i gapel Carmel bob dydd Sul'. If you are asked, 'Fyddet ti'n hoffi mynd i'r eglwys?' the question almost always refers to the church as a building, but if you see a building advertised as 'Eglwys Seion' this could well be a reference to a Seion chapel.

Both 'capel' and 'eglwys' have two plural forms. You might hear, 'Mae llawer o gapeli (llawer o gapelau) yn y dre'. Similarly, you could hear, 'Does dim llawer o eglwysi (llawer o eglwysydd) yn yr ardal'. You can find both 'capel' and 'eglwys' in place-names. There is a Capel Bangor in Ceredigion, and a Capel Curig in Gwynedd. You have Eglwys-fach in Ceredigion and Eglwys Wen in Pembrokeshire.

The first Independent (Puritan) church/chapel in Wales was at Llanfaches, Gwent. It marked the beginning of Nonconformity in Wales. The oldest existing chapel in Wales is Maesyronnen, Powys. It dates from 1696.

Capel Maes-glas, Ysbyty Ystwyth

Eglwys Sant Ioan, Ysbyty Ystwyth

When is a man not a man, I wonder?

The Welsh name for Boudicca, the Queen of the Iceni in the first century, is Buddug. She attacked the Roman army in a revolt outside Londinium when they were attempting to conquer Anglesey. They hurried back and conquered her forces. Buddug took poison and died. There is a statue to her near the Houses of Parliament.

Buddug is often mentioned when reference is made to Welsh heroines, but her battlefield was in eastern Britain at a time when people would not have described themselves as Welsh.

Today, women who strive for equality come across a problem in Welsh. Though the common suffix '-wr' is no more than a grammatical construction, it has masculine connotations and we have 'ffermwr', (farmer), 'gweinyddwr' (administrator), and 'weldiwr' (welder), for example. Despite the fact that 'tafarnwr' (for example) does not refer specifically to a man, all nouns ending in '-wr' are masculine and a sentence such as, 'Aeth y tafarnwr i'r gwely gyda'i gŵr' has a false ring to it.

Because of this, we also have 'gweinyddwraig' and 'pregethwraig' and many other feminine nouns. But many look for a neutral compromise, one such being the suffix '-ydd'. You might read or hear of a firm advertising for a 'gweinyddydd' or a 'weldydd' or 'cyfarwyddydd'. But every noun with the suffix '-ydd' which describes people is masculine, and we have 'ysgrifennydd/ysgrifenyddes', 'organydd/ organyddes', etc . . .

However, many people are eager to popularise '-ydd' as a 'neutral' form and sentences such as 'Gwen yw'r ysgrifennydd newydd', or 'Huw a Gwen yw'r ddau gadeirydd', are quite acceptable.

But you cannot (for example) use 'ffermydd' to describe either a farmer or his wife as '-ydd' can be a plural ending. Furthermore, there is a difference between 'ysgrifennwr' (writer) and 'ysgrifennydd', (secretary). But the use of '-ydd' is becoming more common, with words like 'cricedydd' and 'addysgydd' being adopted. But the problems multiply when plural forms are introduced.

Buddug would not have been happy at being called 'milydd' instead of 'milwr' though she would be happy with 'terfysgydd' (rioter) instead of 'terfysgwr'. The problem is still to be solved satisfactorily.

Taking the wrong line from Merthyr Tudful to Siberia

At one time, those who transgressed in Russia were often sent to Siberia. If they were sent there by train, they could thank a Welshman, John Hughes and his team of Welsh workers, for organising the laying of the first tracks. The Russians were so pleased with his efforts in the nineteenth century industrial revolution that they named a town, Yuzovka after him. If they asked him where he came from, he would say, 'Merthyr Tudful in Wales'.

'Where do you come from?' is a question that is often asked in Wales. We feel easier in conversation if we are familiar with a person's roots. In this respect, the English sentence is happy at having a preposition for a tail. You would sound strange if you asked, 'To where are you going?'

But the Welsh sentence is not happy with a preposition at its rear. Unfortunately, under the influence of English, such a structure is becoming increasingly common in the language. You might well have to respond to someone who asks you, 'Ble rwyt ti'n dod o?' But usually, what you might hear is, 'Ble [rwyt] ti'n dod o?'

This is not good Welsh. The correct structure is, 'O ble'r wyt ti'n dod?' (O ble ti'n dod?). 'Ble mae hi'n dod o?' is also dubious. Similarly, you might hear, 'Ble ti'n mynd i?' The correct structure is, 'I ble'r wyt ti'n mynd?' or, in a shortened form, '(I) Ble ti'n mynd?'

'Pwy wyt ti'n siarad i?' (Â phwy wyt ti'n siarad?), 'Beth wyt ti'n chwilio am?' (Am beth wyt ti'n chwilio?), 'Beth wyt ti'n edrych ar?' (Ar beth wyt ti'n edrych?) are all expressions to be avoided.

As you become more and more familiar with Welsh, remember that a sentence should not end in a preposition. Someone could well suggest wryly that those who transgress should be sentenced to go to Siberia.

A matter of grave concern

One of the most famous of our folk tales is that of Ann Thomas, of Cefnydfa in Glamorgan. Her mother wished her to marry a wealthy lawyer called Maddox, thus solving her financial problems. But Ann wished to marry a poor roofer-minstrel, Wil Hopcyn. She arranged clandestine meetings with him, but her mother found out and confined her to her bedroom. Ann sought to communicate with Wil by writing messages on sycamore leaves, using blood from her arm as ink. She was ultimately compelled to marry the lawyer but her health deteriorated and she died (of a broken heart?) in her lover's arms.

'Ei mam' and 'ei merch' are often contaminated orally by an intrusive 'h', and you might hear, 'Roedd ei mham yn byw yng Nghefnydfa', or 'Mae pen blwydd ei mherch yfory'. With the assistance of this intrusive 'h' the sentence slips more easily off the tongue, but unfortunately it is creeping into written Welsh. Never write, 'Ann oedd enw ei mherch' (merch); or 'Mae ei mham (mam) wedi cael ei phen blwydd'. (Note here that I have printed 'pen blwydd' as two words without a hyphen. It is also correct to hyphenate, 'pen-blwydd', but never write 'penblwydd', bearing in mind that the accent in Welsh is on the penultimate syllable.)

Another intrusive letter is 'i'. You might hear, 'Roedd bron i gant o bobol yno'. The correct form is, 'Roedd bron ddeg o ferched yn y parti pen blwydd'. Here again, the 'i' helps the sentence along orally, but should be omitted from written forms.

You will also meet a 'y', before 'llynedd' (last year). You may well hear and see, 'Es i'r gêm rygbi (y) llynedd', but this particular 'y' is not intrusive, though many people might say, 'Fe ddes i i Gymru llynedd'. It is the correct structure for 'last year'. It is incorrect to say, therefore, 'Es i weld bedd Ann y flwyddyn ddiwethaf'. Say, 'Es i weld y bedd y llynedd'.

Do try to go to Llangynwyd church near Maesteg some day to visit her grave. There are many who will tell you that this harrowing story is true.

Think of that naughty weekend

We are often reminded in Wales about the traditional Sunday (y Sul traddodiadol). We are told that 'diwrnod cyntaf yr wythnos' should be a day of rest with all public houses closed; but this tradition is comparatively young and goes back to slightly over a century. Beyond that time, the traditional Sunday was everything but a day of rest for many. In another sense, it was a day of rest; a rest from a week's arduous toil. Various games would be played, often in the cemeteries, and a visit to the local hostelry to quench one's thirst was common. The church and tavern are often in close proximity.

Linguistically, you might well be bemused by the way we describe the weekend generally. Many people settle for a direct translation from the English and say 'penwythnos'. You might be asked, 'Ble rwyt ti'n mynd ar y penwythnos?'

But others favour a more traditional expression which is older. You might hear, 'Rwy'n mynd fwrw'r Sul'. If you wish to inquire, 'Where are you going to spend the weekend?' you would say, 'Ble (rwyt) ti'n mynd i fwrw'r Sul?' (observe the mutation).

It is traditional for a language to borrow and traditional also for it to observe old forms; so take your pick.

The word 'bwrw' has many meanings, for example, you will come across it when it is raining (bwrw glaw). It can also mean 'imagine'. If you wish to say, 'Imagine that we have plenty of money. We could go to Paris over the weekend', you might say, 'Bwriwch fod digon o arian gyda ni. Gallen ni fynd i Baris fwrw'r Sul'.

To return to 'Bwrw'r Sul', you could also say 'Bwrw'r Nadolig', or 'Bwrw'r Pasg'. If you wish to blame me for giving so many examples, say, 'Rwy'n bwrw'r bai arnoch chi'.

A popular man of the people

One of the most famous Welsh preachers of the eighteenth-century Methodist Revival was Thomas Charles of Bala. Hundreds of people would walk for miles to Bala to hear him preach. He was the foremost developer of the Welsh Sunday School movement that was instrumental in teaching many children and adults to read. He was also actively involved in the distribution of bibles. There is a statue of him in Bala.

People (pobl) is a much used word but you only rarely hear people say 'pobl'. Instead they say 'pobol' with an intrusive 'o' as seen and heard in the title to that popular soap serial, *Pobol y Cwm*.

As the word begins with 'p' it can take the soft, nasal and aspirate mutations. The three operate in this example: 'Mae'r bobol yn gwrando ar fy mhobol i a phobol pobol eraill' (The poeple are listening to my people and the people of other people). But sometimes people go further and foist an additional soft mutation to its mutated form. They might say, 'Roedd llawer o fobol yn gwrando arno'n pregethu'. It is incorrect to say 'fobol' instead of 'bobol' as a letter cannot be mutated twice. This is acute and superfluous treiglophobia.

Though 'pobl' is singular, it has a collective meaning. You may hear people say 'pobl dlawd' or 'pobl dlodion' (poor people). Its plural form, 'pobloedd', is not often used. It takes the soft mutation after the article (y bobloedd). 'Poblog' means 'populous'. Add an '-aidd' to the word and you have the Welsh for 'popular' and you can say, 'Roedd Thomas Charles yn boblogaidd iawn'.

Thomas Charles is reputed to have composed a very effective sales slogan when selling and distributing bibles: 'Beibl i bawb i bobl y byd'. Note the *cynghanedd*.

The fool says that this is a laughing matter

People in eighteenth-century north Wales were often entertained by fools. During the summer months a farm servant, blowing a cracked trumpet to draw attention, might enter a village to announce that an 'anterliwt' (interlude—short play) was to be performed in a certain farmyard. The villagers would postpone any tasks and flock to the 'theatre', a farm cart drawn up in front of a barn (ysgubor)—the dressing-room. They would then be witness to two hours of entertainment in rhyme based on stories like *Dick Whittington*. But their favourite character was the fool, mainly because he could make them laugh. But be careful when you laugh in Welsh.

If you wish to say, 'I laughed at him', the correct idiom is, 'Fe wnes i chwerthin am ('i) ben e(f)'. Note the preposition, 'am' (at). Some people might say (incorrectly), 'Fe wnes i chwerthin ar (e)i ben e' (I laughed on top of him).

The Welsh for 'to laugh' is 'chwerthin'. It is a regular verb but we do strange things with it orally. For example, 'Chwarddodd am ben y ffŵl', means 'He laughed at the ffŵl', but many add an ending to the verb noun and could well say, 'Chwerthinodd am ben y ffŵl'. This incorrect expression is coming more common orally and you can hear expressions like, 'Fe chwerthines i' (I laughed). This is gradually creeping into written Welsh. If you wish to say that you were laughing quietly you would say, 'Rown i'n chwerthin yn fy nwrn'.

People are also prone orally to substitute 'w' for the initial consonant and what you might hear is 'wherthin'. This did not present a problem to most of eighteenth-century south Walians. They listened to sermons about hell instead. Certainly no laughing matter.

John Rowlands, I presume, H M Stanley

Had not H M Stanley gone to Africa to look for him, it is possible that the whereabouts of Dr Livingstone would have remained a mystery. H M Stanley's greeting when they met, 'Dr Livingstone, I presume', is familiar to many. But had someone said to him, 'John Rowlands, I presume', he might well have been annoyed. He wished to gloss over the fact that he was brought up in a workhouse in St Asaph before sailing to America to meet his mentor, Henry Morton Stanley. He wished to erode this chapter in his past from his memory.

I have noted previously that the conditional tense is much used in Welsh and that it often begins with 'Pe . . .' You could say, 'Pe bai Stanley'n cael ei ffordd, byddai'n anghofio am Lanelwy'. (If Stanley had his way, he would . . .). But the structure has been both eroded and usurped.

. A variation of 'Pe bawn i . . .' is 'Pe buaswn i . . .' But in conversation, most of the structure is ignored, and what you might hear is, '(Pe bua)Swn i'n dy le di . . .' For example, ''Swn i'n dy le di, fe fyddwn i'n anghofio am Stanley' (literally: If I were in your place, I would forget about Stanley).

But a different structure altogether beginning with 'Oni bai . . .' is gaining popularity. You might hear, 'Oni bai fy mod i'n gweithio, fe fyddwn i'n mynd i'r gêm' (Were I not working . . .). Here again, beware of oral erosion. You could hear, 'Oni bai (fy) mod i'n gweith'o, 'swn i'n mynd i'r gêm'.

Had Stanley had his wish granted, he would have been buried near Dr Livingstone in Westminster Abbey, but this was not to be. The Dean would not grant his wish and he was buried in Pitbright cemetery, in May 1904.

H M Stanley

A Communist who could relieve toothache on Sunday

One of the founders of the Communist Party in Britain was T E Nicholas, a Welsh-speaking poet-preacher from north Pembrokeshire. He trained for the ministry and ministered in various chapels in Wales but he was unpopular with many because of his strong political, pro Russian views. Because of this opposition, he and his wife learnt the craft of dentistry. Both practised for years in Aberystwyth but Niclas y Glais (as he was known) continued to travel to preach in various chapels on Sundays.

You can suffer toothache in more ways than one in Welsh. Some might inform their dentist, 'Mae dant tost gen i', or 'Mae fy nant i'n dost'. They might use the plural form and say, 'Mae fy nannedd i'n dost', the 'd' mutating to 'n'. People might say generally, 'Mae pen tost gen i', or, 'Mae stumog dost gen i'. This does not mean that they have been standing near a fire for too long. 'Tost' can mean 'sore'. It can also mean 'severe'.

But others might say, 'Mae fy nant i'n gwynio', or 'Mae fy mhen i'n gwynio'. 'Gwynio' means aching; it can also mean 'lusting', but the second expression is almost obsolete. Do not confuse the word either with the Welsh for sewing, which is 'gwnïo' (with an umlaut) with the accent on the 'i'.

Still others might say, 'Mae cur pen gen i', or 'Mae cur yn 'y mhen i', 'cur' being still another word for 'pain'. You could say, 'Mae fy mhen i'n curo', as 'curo' can mean 'throbbing', but this expression is hardly ever used. The most common meaning for 'curo' is 'to beat' or 'to knock', and a child could say, 'Mae'r deintydd yn curo ar y drws'.

T E Nicholas kept his dental equipment in the boot of his car on his Sunday preaching expeditions in case a member of his congregation had a painful tooth during a painful sermon. Better the day . . .

Ladies and gentlemen, water on tap

The man who provided London with its first adequate water supply was a Welshman, Sir Hugh Middleton. He accomplished this feat in 1613, many of his pipes having been constructed from dug out tree trunks. He was a wealthy man and was reputed to be earning £2000 a month from his Ceredigion lead and silver mines. His generosity was a boon for the water closets that were being developed in London around this time.

I have mentioned previously that a water closet is often referred to in Welsh as a 'tŷ bach' and that men and women in north Wales refer to it as 'Lle chwech'.

Today, we are aware of these essential establishments from the symbols placed on them, but you will still see the words 'DYNION' for men and 'GWRAGEDD' or 'MERCHED' or 'BENYWOD' or 'MENYWOD' for women.

The Welsh for 'man' is 'dyn'. It is a very old word. At one time, the Welsh for 'woman' also was 'dyn'. There was no difference. But the word 'dynes' was devised as a colloquial expression to differentiate between male and female. 'Dynes' is a comparatively modern word, merely a few centuries old, and the people who devised it did not appreciate that a plural form would be useful. It was not accepted at the time as a literary form.

Though the dictionary will give you 'dynion' as the plural for 'dyn' you will still find no plural form for 'dynes', so other expressions must be found when drawing attention to utilities such as water closets. You cannot say, 'Mae dynion a dynesion yn y toiled'.

A statue of Sir Hugh Middleton was erected in London to commemorate his generosity. There is no truth in the tale that Ceredigion farmers who went to London to sell milk at the beginning of this century used to lay a wreath annually near this statue to thank him for the gift of water.

If you've got to go, you've got to go

A glance at a map will show that the man-made main roads in north, mid and south Wales go east. All the eighteenth-century drover roads went eastwards and the only motorway that serves Wales does the same. The railway system has followed this pattern, and long before a communication system was built, the major rivers also went towards England. Because of this, it is difficult to develop an unity between north and south Wales; difficult to build a direct, swift route between Caernarfon and Cardiff that would make all kinds of communication easier.

I have mentioned previously that the Welsh for 'to go' is 'mynd'. It is an irregular verb and can cause problems. One of the greatest of these problems is presented by the impersonal form of the past tense. Indeed, all impersonal forms present problems for learners.

The impersonal form of the past tense of 'mynd' offers a choice, 'aed' and 'aethpwyd'. Disregarding the impersonal form, you might hear a news-reader say, 'Aeth yr heddlu â'r lleidr i'r carchar' (The police went with the robber to jail/took the robber to jail). But people might wish to make this statement without reference to the police. What you would hear then would be, 'Aed â'r lleidr i'r carchar'. ('Aethpwyd' is rarely used colloquially but you should be aware of the word.)

But some people disregard 'aed' and say 'awd' instead, e.g., 'Awd â'r plant i'r ysgol'. This is an incorrect form and should be avoided.

The third person imperative personal form also is 'aed' (or 'eled'). You could well hear this form in a play when a king commands, 'Aed ag ef allan!' (Let him be taken out!)

If you could command roads, you might wish to say, 'Aed pob ffordd o'r de i'r gogledd'.

Raining snow and coconuts

The bible was translated into Welsh in 1588. In his translation, Bishop William Morgan gave the Welsh language a wealth of new words and regenerated others, one of his problems being that there were not enough words in living Welsh to convey the language of the bible.

Translating certain words into different languages can present strange problems. It would seem to be straightforward to translate 'White as the driven snow' into any language, but when confronted with the bible in their language, people in the South Sea Islands inquired, 'What is snow?' The translators had to compromise and say, 'The flesh of the coconut'. Grønland presented a somewhat different problem. The Inuit use at least forty different words to describe snow, and their inquiry was, 'What kind of snow?'

We have many means of describing the weather in Welsh. Describing 'snowing' is straightforward. We say, 'Mae'n bwrw eira'. If the snow is drifting, we say, 'Mae'n lluwchio'. Our word for 'sleet' is 'eirlaw' (eira + glaw). There is a more comprehensive list to say that it is raining. Some simply say, 'Mae'n bwrw glaw'. Others say, 'Mae'n glawio'. If it's raining cats and dogs in English, we use the expression, 'Mae'n bwrw hen wragedd a ffyn'. We refer to 'drizzle' as 'glaw mân', or 'briwlaw'. But we also have words to describe random drops of rain falling. Some might say, 'Mae'n smwcian', but others refer to this as 'briwlan', keeping 'glaw mân' for drizzle. When we wish to refer to showers, we say, 'Mae'n bwrw cawodydd', or 'Mae'n cawodi'. Some people substitute 'f' for 'w' and say 'cafodydd' (cafodydd Ebrill = April showers). If it looks like rain listen for, 'Mae hi'n hel at law'. If it is hailing, some might say, 'Mae'n bwrw cenllysg', but others might say, 'Mae'n bwrw ceser' (a colloquialism for 'cesair').

It is useful to know them all, but there is no record of the South Sea Islanders having inquired, 'What kind of coconut?'

Open and shut case of the vanishing valley

Around 1850, the population of Rhondda was under 1,000. The first coal-mine was opened around that time and soon people from all over Wales were settling in the valley. By 1871, the population had risen to 20,000. It was 112,000 by the end of the century. Many shops, chapels, churches, public houses and community halls were opened.

But things have changed. Coal-mines have been shut and in their wake the chapels, churches and community halls also have been shut. By 1985, the population had shrunk to 78,700 and the figures are going down annually.

'Agor' and 'cau' are amongst the first Welsh words you come across when learning Welsh. When a shop is open, you might see 'Ar Agor' displayed on the door. Sometimes you might see 'Agored' which means much the same thing. When a shop is shut, you might see two forms, 'Ar Gau' (the most common) and also 'Yng Nghau' (yn + cau—with a nasal mutation) which also means much the same thing.

But these two words have other meanings as well. 'Cau' can mean 'empty' and the Welsh for 'hollow tree' is 'coeden gau'. If you feel rude and you wish someone to 'shut up', you would say, 'Cau dy geg', though to be strictly correct, you should write 'Cae dy geg' (third person, singular, the imperative mood of 'cau').

'Agor' can also mean 'expand/open out' and you can say, 'Roedd Cwm Rhondda'n agor o'n blaen'. If you feel sleepy you might yawn, or 'ymagor' (ym + agor) and in north Wales you do not often use a key to lock a door. If you have lost the key, you might ask, 'Wyt ti wedi gweld yr agoriad?' To south Walians, 'agoriad' means 'an opening'.

Before the pits were dug a squirrel could hop from tree to tree all the way from Blaenrhondda to the outskirts of Cardiff and hear Welsh spoken all the way.

Be awake to the call of the trumpet

In 1993 the National Eisteddfod was held at Llanelwedd, the first time for it to visit the old Radnorshire. A few of the Eisteddfodwyr went on a pilgrimage towards the sometime home of the Scudamore family on the boundary between Herefordshire and Radnorshire. One of the daughters of Owain Glyndŵr married into this family and the area would have been well known to her father. Though nobody knows for certain where Owain is buried, one tradition tells us that he fled here after his last battle against the English and that his grave is in the locality.

Another tradition tells us that he is not dead but that he is sleeping somewhere near the slopes of Cefn Cennarth. Like Arthur, he will awake to the call of the trumpet on the day he thinks that Wales needs him.

Linguistically, we wake up in different ways in different parts of Wales. You could hear some people say, 'Rwy'n deffro am saith bob dydd'. Others might say, 'Rwy'n dihuno cyn newyddion chwech bob dydd'. 'Deffro' has retained its original structure in its written form, but in conversation, many people might say, 'Rwy'n dino (d(ihu)no) sawl gwaith yn y nos'.

Most people, if they wish to say that they were awake early, would say, 'Rown i ar ddi-hun am wyth y bore 'ma'. If they tell you, 'Rown i'n effro drwy'r ddarlith', expect an overtone of being very much awake, and not sleepy.

'Hun' forms a part of the Welsh for 'nightmare' and someone might say, 'Fe ges i hunlle(f) gas neithiwr'.

People at the Eisteddfod in Llanelwedd were very much awake during the main Gorsedd ceremonies, but a few patriots were concerned that the sleeping Owain Glyndŵr could well have been confused by the trumpet calls.

A happy radio signal from Wales

In Lavernock church outside Cardiff there is this inscription: Near this spot the first radio messages were exchanged across water by Guglielmo Marconi and George Kemp between Lavernock and Flat Holm 11th May . . . 1897.

Many scientists could not accept that Marconi could transmit radio messages. Fortunately, William Preece, a Welshman from Bontnewydd outside Caernarfon, who worked for British Telegraph, believed in him and contributed towards the costs of his experiments and also helped him in other ways.

A Welsh preposition for 'towards' is 'tua' (before a consonant) or 'tuag' (before a vowel). You would say, 'Tua Bangor' but 'Tuag Aberystwyth'. Another preposition for 'towards' is 'at'. As both have the same meaning, there is no need to pair them always, either in writing or in conversation. You sometimes hear on the media, 'Mae'n cyfrannu tuag at bob achos da', but here it is sufficient to say, to quote another example, 'Mae'n cyfrannu at Gymorth Cristnogol' (Christian Aid).

If you say to a child, 'Dos at y drws' (not 'i'r drws'), you expect him to go to the door, but if you say, 'Dos tuag at y car', you expect him to go towards the car, or to approach it.

I have mentioned 'at' before and I have stated that it is being eroded gradually from the language as so many people use 'i' (the translation of the English, 'to') instead of it. You do not say, 'ychwanegu llaeth i'r te' but 'ychwanegu llaeth at y te'. Never say, 'Rwy'n sgrifennu iddo fe', but 'Rwy'n sgrifennu ato fe'. 'Daeth at y ffenest(r)' means, 'He came to the window'. On the other hand, 'Daeth i'r ffenest' means, 'He came into the window'. 'Daeth tuag at y pentre' means that he came in the direction of the village.

A week after his first experiment, Marconi aimed his radio signals towards Weston-super-Mare. In 1897, this was something of a miracle. We should remember this when we look at (or look towards) our radio set.

1897   1947

NEAR THIS SPOT
THE FIRST RADIO MESSAGES
WERE EXCHANGED ACROSS WATER
BY
GUGLIELMO MARCONI
AND
GEORGE KEMP
BETWEEN LAVERNOCK & FLAT HOLM 11ᵗᴴ MAY,
LAVERNOCK & BREAN DOWN 18ᵗᴴ MAY 1897
ERECTED BY THE ROTARY CLUB OF CARDIFF 1947

Eglwys Larnog a'r gofeb i waith Marconi

There are no gun slinging bards in the Gorsedd

During the first week in August, the National Eisteddfod is a 'must' for many people. The National Anthem will be heard during all the main ceremonies and at the end of every session. Patriotism will abound.

One of the visitors at the Blaenau Ffestiniog Eisteddfod in 1898 was Goscombe John, a famous sculptor in his day. It was he who designed the memorial to Evan and James James at Ynysangharad Park, Pontypridd, to commemorate the composing of 'Hen Wlad fy Nhadau'. He was also responsible for the statue of Daniel Owen, the famous nineteenth-century novelist, in Mold. He was much impressed by the dignified Gorsedd ceremony and designed the horn of plenty (y corn hirlas) for it. This horn is borne and offered to the archdruid by one of the married ladies of the eisteddfod locality.

The modern gorsedd members are attired in green, blue and white robes. The Welsh for robes is 'gynau'. Note that the word is spelt with a single 'n'. If you double the 'n', you have another entirely different, but commonly used word with two different meanings. If you write, 'Roedd y beirdd yn gwisgo gynnau', you are stating that the bards were carrying guns as 'gynnau' can be the plural for 'gwn', but if you say, 'Fe welais i'r archdderwydd gynne (gynnau)', you are stating that you saw the archdruid not so long ago. If you wish to say that you have just seen the horn of plenty, you would say, 'Fe weles i'r corn hirlas gynne (gynnau) fach'. This is a shorter period of time. People often say, 'Roedd e 'ma gynne fach'.

Many are concerned that the Gorsedd procession is not as dignified as it used to be. People in their gowns talk to onlookers. They do not process properly. Gorsedd leaders would like to cure this problem. If you say on the eisteddfod field, 'Mae gynnau gwyn gan y beirdd', people could well believe that drastic measures are being taken by the archdruid to rectify this.

Thereby hangs a ruby rope

Thomas Edwards was the last person to be hanged for murder in Merionethshire. Because he hailed from south Wales, he was nicknamed 'Yr Hwntw Mawr'. In 1813, he was working on the Cob in Porthmadog and discovered that valuables were kept in a cupboard in Penrhyn Isaf farm nearby. When he thought the coast was clear, he broke into the house but was confronted by the maid, Mary Jones. He killed her, broke open the cupboard and went away with valuables, hiding them in a sheep-fold. He went to a well to wash the blood from his hands and in Welsh it is still known as 'Ffynnon yr Hwntw Mawr'. When he returned to the fold to collect his booty, he was spotted, caught and brought to justice.

The Welsh for 'murderer' is 'llofrudd'. You could hear, 'Yr Hwntw Mawr oedd y llofrudd'. It can split into two separate words, llof + rhudd. Years ago, the Welsh for 'hand' was 'llawf' but the 'f' was dropped and we have 'llaw'. 'Rhudd' is a form of red, but do not confuse the word with 'rhydd' (spelt differently) which means 'free'. In this instance, there is a suggestion that a murderer's hand is red with the blood of his victim.

You will hardly ever hear 'rhudd' used by itself but it is used as a verb when a person is ironing. If he wishes to say that a cloth has scorched, he would say, 'Mae'r llien (lliain) wedi rhuddo'.

Another word for 'cheek' is 'grudd' (plural = gruddiau). It is also found in the Welsh translation for 'ruby'. A ruby wedding is 'priodas ruddem' (rhudd + gem) the 'rh' being mutated. You could say, 'Roedd modrwy ruddem am ei bys hi'. At one time, girls were not happy at having a 'ruby' set in a ring. They thought that it was an omen of blood on their hands.

Being contented with the advantage of bilingualism

One of the most eccentric characters in Wales at the beginning of the last century was Richard Robert Jones, known as Dic Aberdaron, after his birthplace. He did not wish to follow his father as a boat builder and was quite content learning languages. He learnt Latin when he was twelve and later learnt Greek, Hebrew, Spanish, Italian, and English. He left home when he was a teenager and was happy travelling around Britain, carrying books in the folds of his clothes. He would sell a few occasionally in order to buy food. Later on, he would buy them back. A contented cat accompanied him on his travels.

If you wish to say that you are contented in Welsh, you would say, 'Rwy i wrth (f)y modd'. Dic would have said, 'Rwy i wrth 'y modd yn dysgu ieithoedd'. If you wish to say that he was contented playing in the sand, you would say, 'Roedd e wrth 'i fodd yn chwar(a)e yn y tywod' (note the mutation). If you wish to say that you and a friend were contented in a concert, you would say, 'Roedden ni wrth yn (ein) bodd yn y cyngerdd'. You will find that sometimes in conversation, people will use a plural form of 'bodd' (boddau/bodde) and say, 'Roedden ni wrth ein bodde yn yr haul'. This is quite unnecessary. It is correct to say, 'Fe fyddwch chi i gyd wrth eich bodd yn dysgu Cymraeg'.

But beware of the mutated form, 'modd' as it can also mean 'means'. You could say, 'Siarad llawer â phobol yw'r modd gore o ddysgu Cymraeg'. If a person is poor you could say, 'Does dim llawer o fodd ganddo fe'.

There is no truth in the story that the cat could bark as well as mew, being aware of the advantages of bilingualism.

Tall and not so tall meanings to ponder over in a pub

Before the boundary changes, one of the tallest structures in Wales was to be found in its smallest county. It is the chimney of St Athan Power Station in the Vale of Glamorgan, which brings me to a simple word that can confuse the learner. This is 'tal', the Welsh for 'tall'. But when 'tal' takes the soft mutation it becomes 'dal', a word that you might not find in dictionaries. I mentioned sentences you might hear on page 84. If you wish to say that a person is very tall, you would simply say, 'Mae e'n dal iawn'. If you wish to avoid the mutation, say, 'Dyn tal ydy e'. If you want to go a step further and say that a person is tall and strong, you may use a composite word and say, 'Mae e'n dalgryf iawn'. I mentioned on page 84 also that 'dal' can also mean 'to catch'. There is too a common idiom which might be used by someone suffering from a cold, 'Rwy i 'di dal annwyd'.

But 'dal' can also mean 'to continue'. A person might ask you, 'Wyt ti'n dal i fyw yn y pentre?' or he might ask simply, 'Wyt ti'n dal yma?' (Are you still here—continuing to be here?)

It can also mean 'to hold'. If you are holding on desperately to something and someone urges you not to let go, he might shout, 'Dal dy af(a)el' (Hold your grip). Similarly, he might say, 'Dal dy ana(d)l' (Hold your breath), when he is about to undertake a daring task.

Furthermore it can mean 'to contain'. You could say, 'Mae'r jwg fawr yn dal peint o ddŵr'.

There is a tiny fourteenth-century public house near the Aberddawan chimney. Many a tall story has been told in this once isolated hostelry over the years, but never say 'stori dal' in Welsh.

Look carefully at me, and you will see

A few old Welsh churches have what may be described as peeping holes or spy holes in the side of the chancel. People standing outside could look through these holes at the priest taking a service. When the churches were being erected the church authorities would not have been too happy with the knowledge that people with mortally infectious diseases could well be mixing with the congregation, but they were quite happy to have these slits provided in the walls so that they could look, even if they could not take part.

People use the affirmative, 'look', fairly soon when learning Welsh, but you can be commanded to look in many ways. The Welsh for the affirmative 'Look' is 'Edrych'. The expression is very popular, but in conversation, many people will (quite wrongly) add an 'a' and drop the initial 'E'. What you will hear is, 'Drycha!' A sentence would be, 'Drycha arna i'.

People might well use another command, 'Sbia'. This can mean, 'Look' or 'Spy'. 'Sbia arna i nawr', is a common expression. When you are writing 'sbia' there is no need for an umlaut over the 'i'.

In some parts of the country, people might well use a completely different word, 'Disgwyl', which has three different meanings: look, expect, wait.

If we wish to be strictly correct, we would say, 'Disgwyl arna i' or 'Disgwyliwch arna i', in the affirmative, but in the second person singular, people will again add an 'a' and they will ignore the first two letters, and what you might hear would be, 'Sgwyla' (or 'Sgwylwch') arna i'.

It is rumoured that quite healthy people in Ceredigion preferred looking through peepholes to sitting in the nave during services as by so doing, they would be avoiding the collection plate.

Don't go out of your way to be out

Traditionally, people used to celebrate the new year by holding a 'Noson Gyflaith' (Toffee Evening). Neighbours would be invited to a feast of goose and Christmas pudding followed by games, story telling and 'tynnu cyfleth' (pulling toffee). A mixture of brown sugar, salty butter and water would have been boiling in a saucepan on the fire for some time. When ready it would be poured on to a stone slab and left outside to cool. It would then be brought in, pulled into long, yellow-brown ribbons and consumed with relish.

The Welsh for 'outside' is 'allan' but the word can be used in various ways. Simply, 'Rhoi'r cyfleth allan i oeri', means, 'Putting the toffee out to cool'. People sometimes quarrelled over this. 'Roedden nhw'n cwympo allan', but 'allan' is often used unnecessarily. Someone might say, 'Mae'r tân wedi mynd allan', borrowing from the English, 'The fire has gone out', but a better expression is, 'Mae'r tân wedi diffodd'. You might hear on the media, 'Maen nhw wedi colli allan', but an adequate Welsh expression would be, 'Maen nhw wedi colli'r cyfle'. If we wish to say that a breed is becoming extinct, we would say, 'Maen nhw'n darfod o'r tir'. Do not say, 'Maen nhw'n marw allan'. If you cannot understand a sentence, do not say, 'Rwy'n methu gneud y frawddeg allan'. Say instead, 'Rwy'n methu deall y frawddeg'. Never say, 'Rydw i allan o laeth', but 'Does dim llaeth gen i'. Don't say, 'Maen nhw'n well allan yn y tŷ newydd', but, 'Maen nhw'n well 'u byd yn y tŷ newydd'.

Never translate an English idiom if you have a Welsh one that will suffice.

Sometimes, toffee makers would not be able to enjoy their 'cyfleth' (a word that is rarely used today). They would put it out to cool not realising that a few would be on the prowl looking for something for nothing. It was important to post a lookout who did not have a sweet tooth when toffee was being cooled—just in case they lost out.

Looks at the locks as quickly as possible before the end

Hundreds of people converged on Pen-twyn (Pendine) sands on 3 March 1927. They had come to see Parry Thomas break the world record in his car, Babs, a car that could travel very quickly at that time. It was a fine day and the sand was as smooth as an ironed tablecloth. The record to be broken was 174 mph. He was required to go very quickly along a measured mile in both directions, his speed being averaged. But whilst he was on his first run the driving chain snapped and the car rolled over. Parry Thomas was killed.

You could well be confused by a very common command in Welsh, 'Dere 'ma, glou!' (Come here quickly!) You will not find the adjective 'clou' in the dictionary as the correct spelling is 'clau'. The command should therefore be, 'Dere 'ma glau', but all of us adopt an idiomatic 'glou' in conversation. The unmutated form is hardly ever used.

. But you must not confuse 'clau' with the verb noun, 'cloi' which means 'to lock'. You could well hear, 'Rhaid iti gloi'r drws glou'. The Welsh for 'locked' is 'ar glo' or 'ynghlo' (yn + clo). You can take your choice here in a sentence such as, 'Mae'r drws ar glo/ynghlo, 'dw i'n meddwl'. If we wish to terminate a debate, we would say, 'Rhaid inni gloi'r ddadl nawr'. The Welsh word for 'conclusion' is 'diweddglo'— with a 'lock' at the end. You might hear, 'Mae diweddglo trist i'r nofel'.

The spelling is crucial here as there is still another word, 'clai', which means 'clay'. A clay pipe would be 'pibell glai', the 'c' mutating. 'A clay pigeon shoot', would be, 'Saethu colomennod clai'.

Babs was buried at Pen-twyn (Pendine) after the accident but after many years it was dug up and painstakingly restored to be a showpiece in a museum. Ond dydy e ddim yn gallu mynd yn glau iawn heddiw.

Parry Thomas ac eraill gyda'r car, Babs

A song to control a crowd

The summer of 1966 was a momentous one for Plaid Cymru. Gwynfor Evans was elected to parliament and everybody was elated. On the night of the count hundreds of his supporters had assembled in Carmarthen town. Rival parties were there as well and there were a few heated arguments. The police officer in charge of crowd control was concerned that things could get out of hand, but he had an inspired idea. He stood on the balcony of the town hall and shouted, 'Pawb i ganu!' Everybody (well, nearly everybody) sang for hours under his conductorship.

The Welsh for 'everybody' is 'pawb'. At one time people looked upon it as a singular pronoun. A proverbial remark that you might well hear during an argument might be, 'Rhydd i bawb ei farn' (Everyone is entitled to his (or her) opinion). It is sometimes expressed as, 'Rhydd i bob un ei farn'. Another common expression is, 'Pawb at y peth y bo' (Each to his own)—a singular form.

To be strictly correct, 'Pawb i ganu!' means, 'Every *one* to sing!' but you could hear as well, 'Pawb i ddod erbyn deg a dewch â brechdane (sandwiches) gyda chi' (Everybody to come . . .). Here, it has a plural form, and it would appear unnatural for someone to say, 'a dere â brechdane gyda thi'. We expect the plural here.

But if a tutor asks in a class, 'Ydy pawb wedi cyrraedd?' or 'Ydy pob un wedi cyrraedd?', he/she is asking if every single person has arrived. Whether 'pawb' is singular or plural depends on what you wish to say.

'Pob' crops up also when we refer to things and places. We would say, 'Mae'n gwybod pob dim', or 'Mae'n mynd i bob man'. But in certain situations, the two words are joined, for example, 'Mae popeth yn iawn', or, 'Mae'n mynd i bobman'. Note that the final 'b' of 'pob' is subsumed in the initial 'p' of 'popeth'.

People sometimes separate the two words if they wish to emphasise a point, 'Ma'r babi'n mynd i *bob* man'.

Making a meal of pancakes and Welsh cakes

The custom of making Welsh cakes goes back well over a century. They were easy to make and were popular in farmhouses and cottages. The collier used to take them with him underground. Pancakes were a different matter. On Shrove Tuesday, the remainder of the butter that had been stored over winter would be used. It would be mixed with a few of the eggs collected around the houses by children (a custom that has died out), together with flour and buttermilk. This was a feast for the people before the fast of Lent.

You will come across the Welsh name for Welsh cakes in various forms, but one of the most common is 'pice mân'. A hardly ever used Welsh word for 'bun' is 'picen', but 'pice' is the colloquial form of the plural, 'picau'. Do not be confused by 'mân'. In this instance, it does not mean 'small'. It is a colloquialism for the 'maen' (stone) which is placed above the fire—a baking stone. 'Pice mân', therefore, is a corruption of 'picau ar y maen'.

Sometimes a griddle would be used, and people might describe them as 'pice radell' or 'teisenne radell'. Here the Welsh for griddle (gradell) has lost the initial 'g' in mutation. Other common expressions are 'pice bach' or 'cage bach' (small cakes).

We usually use the Welsh forms of English words to describe pancakes. In mid Wales, a housewife might say, 'Rwy'n gneud powncage heddi' (pown = pan). Others prefer the word 'crempog'. This is the Welsh form of the English, 'crumpet' but in the Swansea valley, they might ask you, 'Wyt ti'n leicio ffroes?'—sometimes incorrectly spelt as 'ffrois'.

Remember that the Welsh for 'buttermilk' in south Wales is 'llaeth enwyn'. In north Wales, it is called 'llaeth', the Welsh for 'milk' being 'llefrith'.

The modern birthday is not complete without a 'teisen' (cacen) ben blwydd. Years ago, pancakes were the birthday treat, much cheaper and much more filling.

A *hundred, a plot of land and a century*

One of the most famous Welsh kings was Hywel Dda. He is reputed to have been the first to codify Welsh laws in Whitland in the tenth century (y ddegfed ganrif). If you visit the town, you will see a beautifully set out memorial garden to him by Peter Lord. A word for 'district' that appears in these laws is 'cantref'. It was used years ago to describe around a hundred homes or large farms. Part of the word is still to be seen in 'cartref' (home), 'pentref' (village) and 'tref' (town).

The Welsh word 'cant' for 'hundred' should present no problems, but it can cause confusion in its mutated forms. You might hear, 'Mae gan Hywel gan punt'. The two words 'gan', though spelt the same ('cant' taking an initial soft mutation and losing its ultimate 't') have different meanings. But if you wish to say that Hywel's wife has a similar amount, you would say, 'a chan(t) punt gan ei wraig hefyd'. Here, 'cant' takes the aspirant mutation.

Again, you could hear, '. . . a chânt gwpan a chant o bunnoedd yn wobr'. In such an example, the circumflex can be an indicator.

Another way of writing 'a chant o bunnoedd' would be, 'a chan punt'. Remember to keep to the singular. You cannot say, 'a chan punnoedd'.

The plural for 'cant' is 'cannoedd', but in conversation, the 'e' is often dropped and you have 'canno(e)dd'. Note that the final 'nt' becomes 'nn'. The doubling of the consonant could be a useful indicator in a construction such as, 'Fe ganodd e'r gân ganno(e)dd o weithie'.

When a person is 100 years old, you could say, 'Ma' fe'n gant oed', or, 'Ma' fe'n gan mlwydd oed'. Here 'blwydd(yn)' takes the soft mutation after 'gan'.

Nobody refers to Hywel Dda's 'cantref' (hundred) nowadays.

A pirate who plundered the Spanish

One of the most famous pirates in Stuart times was a Welshman called Henry (Harri) Morgan. He went to Jamaica to seek his fortune and King Charles was happy for him to steal gold and silk from the Spanish ships on their way home from Brazil. In 1664, he was made deputy governor of Jamaica and a 'sir' to boot. Seven years later he captured and plundered Panama. He was buried in a seaside grave in Port Royal, Jamaica.

A reporter could have said of the buccaneer, 'Roedd e'n dwyn aur y Sbaenwyr ac yn dwyn y cyfan i Jamaica' (He was stealing the gold of the Spaniards and taking it all to Jamaica). 'Dwyn' is a word to be wary of. The above example shows that it can mean, amongst other things, 'steal' or 'bring'. 'Mae Harri wedi dwyn arian o'r siop', suggests that Harri is a thief, but 'Mae'r heddlu wedi dwyn achos yn erbyn Harri', states that he will be brought before his betters.

The third person singular of 'dwyn' is 'dygodd'. You could say, 'Fe ddygodd e'r arian i gyd'. An expression with a colloquial flavour would be, 'Mae Harri wedi dygyd (or dwgyd) yr arian'. But in conversation, some people might well say, 'Fe ddwynodd Harri'r sidan (silk) i gyd'. In this instance, they would be trespassing on still another oral corruption, 'dwyno', which means to make dirty. The verb noun here is 'difwyno' but the 'if' is usually lost in conversation. In the above example, Harri could either have stolen the silk or dirtied it.

You can always avoid the problem by using the word 'lladrata' for 'to steal', but though it is common as a verb noun it is rarely used as a verb. In the third person, we would say, 'Fe ddygodd e'r sidan i gyd'.

The ocean waves had the last laugh on Harri Morgan. During a storm they pounded the cemetery and stole his body, taking it back to the sea he loved.

Be wary of the little words and crafty saints

We often refer to the British Isles as Great Britain (Prydain Fawr). Sometimes, the Great is dropped, often by people who no longer think that the adjective 'great' is justified, but at one time many referred to Brittany in northern France as Prydain Fach (Little Britain). The 'great' and the 'little' would have been important at that time to differentiate between the two countries.

Welsh saints established monastic settlements in Britanny. One of the biggest was dedicated to Teilo, who is often depicted on a stag. The innocent people of Britanny offered him as much land as he could go around in one day for a monastery. They were duped.

'They' (hwy) is an important pronoun to be wary of in Welsh because of the way it has developed in oral forms. A literary form would be, 'maent hwy' (they are), but the final 't' has mutated to 'nh' and has 'moved over' as it were to 'hwy', which in turn has dropped its ultimate 'y'. You should hear, 'Maen nhw' in a sentence such as, 'Maen nhw wedi mynd ers amser', but the final two letters of 'maen' and the 'h' of 'nhw' are also often dropped and what you hear is, 'Ma nw (we)di gorffen nawr'.

You hardly ever hear 'hwy' in conversation but it is often used in sermons and sometimes by news-readers. If you turn to books of grammar, you will hardly ever see 'nhw' described (with 'hwy, hwynt') as an independent third person plural pronoun.

Though you can safely disregard 'hwy' in conversation, and concentrate on 'nhw', you must be aware of the form as it is very common in literary Welsh. 'Nhw' is also very much in evidence and could well supersede 'hwy' in time.

When Teilo was invited to 'go' around a tract of land, he went on the back of a stag. That is why he secured so much land. So be wary of little words.

Always be certain of what it takes to steal

On page 121 I referred to a famous Welsh buccaneer in relation to the word 'dwyn'. Another famous buccaneer was Bartholomew Roberts from Pembrokeshire, known generally as Barti Ddu. Early in the eighteenth century he sailed towards a fleet of 42 Portuguese ships, noted which one carried most treasure, boarded it and took it away. Because of this daring deed, and others, he was feared everywhere. When he entered Newfoundland harbour, the crews of 22 ships took flight. He was killed in a sea battle and was buried at sea dressed in all his finery.

The verb noun for 'to take' is 'cymryd'. Many people introduce an internal (but intrusive) 'e' in conversation, and say 'cymeryd'. This is not correct. But on the other hand, the Welsh verb for 'he/she took' is 'cymerodd' (with an internal 'e'). We could have, therefore, 'Roedd Barti Ddu'n cymryd trysor y llongau', or, 'Fe gymerodd Barti Ddu drysor y llongau'.

'Cymryd' is often, but not always, interchangeable with 'dwyn'. 'Dwyn' is more commonly used in parts of north Wales. 'Cymerodd' is common in a few popular idioms. The Welsh for 'He/she took for granted', is 'Cymerodd yn ganiataol'. Another useful phrase is, 'Mae'n cymryd arno', for example, 'Mae'n cymryd arno'i fod e'n sâl' (He fakes that he is unwell).

But the meaning can be clouded in conversation. A mother could ask her child, 'Gymerest ti'r arian?' Such a phrase has to be examined in its context. It could be that the mother is suspecting her child of having aspirations to being a buccaneer or merely affirming that he has his school dinner money.

It is said that it was Barti Ddu who devised the flag with the skull and crossbones on it, to warn unlucky sailors that he was about to take their treasures or their ships.

Sometimes things can be most, most strange

We are familiar with the seven wonders of the ancient world, but Wales has its own seven wonders. The most famous of these is Pistyll Rhaeadr, a waterfall near Llanrhaeadr-ym-Mochnant, where William Morgan is reputed to have translated most of the bible into Welsh. This feat is more of a wonder than the waterfall. Very often, the flow of water leaves much to be desired but the views when it is frozen can be magnificent. A hard winter could therefore be the best time for a visit.

The Welsh for 'wonder' is 'rhyfeddod'. If we are captivated by something, we would say, 'Mae e'n ddigon o ryfeddod'. The verb noun is 'rhyfeddu' (to wonder, to marvel). This is commonly used in conversation. If somebody surprises one by his or her actions, you might hear, 'Rwy'n rhyfeddu ato fe/ati hi'. One Welsh statement for 'I'm not surprised', would be, 'Dw i'n rhyfeddu dim!'

If someone betrays slight mental quirks, and is, in common English parlance, 'a bit weak in the head', you might hear someone say, 'Mae e wedi mynd yn rhyfedd'. In parts of Wales, you might well hear, 'Mae wic arno fe', 'wic' being a distorted translation of 'weak'.

Words and phrases are often distorted out of recognition in conversation, 'i'w ryfeddu', being one such phrase. If you wish to say that someone or something is exceptionally good, you could say, 'Mae e'n dda iawn'. A few people might say, quite unnecessarily, 'Mae e'n dda iawn, iawn, iawn'. Others might say (colloquially), 'Mae e'n dda i'r feddu', or if a person has gone a bit strange, 'Mae e wedi mynd yn rhyfedd i'r feddu', Not all people are aware that they are distorting 'i'w ryfeddu', when they say 'i'r feddu'.

South Walians are not too happy about our seven wonders as they all seem to be in north Wales. No wonder they are annoyed!

Pistyll Rhaeadr, Llanrhaeadr-ym-Mochnant

A continuing matter of brown bread and cheese

The greatest Welsh industrialist of the nineteenth century was David Davies, Llandinam, Montgomeryshire. He was chiefly responsible for developing Rhondda valley coal-mines and when he could not ship the 'black gold' satisfactorily through Cardiff Docks, he built his own docks at Barry. When he was opening Barry Docks, he reminded his audience that it was important to learn English to get on in the world and said, 'If you wish to eat brown bread, speak Welsh but if you wish to eat white bread like me, speak English'. At this time, white flour was expensive to refine and buy.

The Welsh for bread is 'bara' and the initial 'b' mutates when you buy a loaf of bread, 'Torth o fara'. When you wish to buy white bread you ask for 'bara gwyn', but if you wish to ask for a white loaf, the feminine form of the adjective is used and you say, 'torth wen'. A bakery is referred to as a bread shop: 'Siop fara'.

But don't think of bread every time you see the word 'bara'. The Welsh verb noun for 'to continue' is 'parhau'. You will often see 'I'w barhau' (To be continued) in print. 'Parhau' is being superseded by 'para'. You might hear, 'Mae'n para i fwrw glaw'. This form appears in our dictionaries and is seen regularly in written forms. In certain instances, the initial 'p' mutates and the word becomes 'bara'. You might hear, 'Ydy'r bara'n mynd i bara am ddeuddydd?'

The Welsh for laver bread at one time was 'bara lafwr', but the 'f' has disappeared in conversation and we have 'bara lawr' which bears no relationship to our loaf.

If we wish to say that a person is earning a living, we would say, 'Mae'n ennill 'i fara caws yn yr ysgol/yn y ffatri'. Here, 'bara caws' (bread and cheese) does not refer to salary.

History has caused David Davies's anecdote to fall rather flat. Today, you can eat brown bread and earn a vast amount of bread and cheese.

A wage of mead, with no pinch of salt

The first example of Welsh poetry does not occur in Wales but in a district described as Yr Hen Ogledd (The Old North) around present day Edinburgh (Caeredin). The name of the poet was Aneirin and his work, 'Canu Aneirin', is to be found in a manuscript written around 1250. The poem describes three hundred soldiers travelling south on the Roman road to Catterick (Catraeth) near Leeds to fight the Saxons. It states that they fought against 50,000 Saxons, a figure to be taken with a pinch of salt.

Your introduction to the first structures of Welsh was probably in an evening class somewhere in Wales but the first structures that you learnt depended on which part of Wales the class was. Take for example the Welsh for, 'I am going'. The full (and almost obsolete) literary construction is, 'Yr ydwyf i'n mynd'. Nobody would say such a sentence. What you hear today are shortened versions, again, depending on where you live. If you attend an Wlpan course, you might well have learnt, '(Y)R ydw(yf) i'n mynd = (Rydw i'n)'. In north Wales, on the other hand, you might have learnt '(Yr y)Dw(y)f i'n mynd = (Dw i'n)', but in west Wales, you might learn, '(Y)R (yd)wy(f i)'n mynd = (Rwy'n)'. But some evening classes might have taught you '(Yr yd)W(y) i'n mynd = (Wi'n)'.

You must be aware of all these forms, but indigenous Welsh speakers tend to 'ignore' them and concentrate on the verb noun— here, 'mynd'. If you wish to express 'I went', you could say, 'Es i', 'Mi es i' (generally, north Wales) or 'Fe es i' (generally, west Wales). Again, just concentrate on the 'Es' but be aware of the various constructions.

The three hundred soldiers from the Old North were nearly all slain by the Saxons. Roman soldiers were paid in salt (salary) but whilst in training, the Caeredin soldiers were paid in fresh 'medd' (mead). The poet says that this 'medd' was metaphorically a poison (gwenwyn) to them. No wonder.

You cannot be friendly with blood on your hand

Owain ap Thomas ap Rhodri was a mercenary. The 'ap' (or ab) means 'the son of'. The Welsh for 'son' is 'mab' but the 'm' has disappeared here and the 'b' has hardened to 'p'. This was the custom of naming in Wales before surnames were introduced. Owain would have been well known in the European community in the fourteenth century. He was born in Surrey and spent much of his time fighting with the French army. One historian described him as 'possibly the greatest military genius Wales has produced'. His nickname was Owain Lawgoch.

He could well have had this name because he had blood on his hand. I mention on page 111 that a murderer was known as 'llofrudd' (= llaw rudd = red hand). You will be familiar with one way in which 'hand' is used in Welsh, 'help llaw' being 'a helping hand'. If we wish to say something in passing, we would say, 'gyda llaw', for example, 'Gyda llaw, fydda i ddim yno heno'. You will know that 'llaw dde' means 'right hand' but if you join the two words, you have the Welsh for 'dexterous', in a sentence such as, 'Roedd Owain yn llawdde gyda'i fwa (bow)'. You will know that 'llaw chwith' means 'left hand', but if you are given 'help llaw chwith', it means that you are being assisted unwillingly. You will know that 'dwylo' (dwy + llaw, not 'llawiau') means two hands, but if you say, 'Doedd Owain ddim yn llawiau gyda'r Saeson', you are saying that he was not friendly with the English.

This proved to be his downfall, really. The people of Wales thought that Owain Lawgoch would come one day to free them from the English aggressor and he was assembling an army to do just that, but a Scotsman was paid £200 by the English government for murdering him near Bordeaux in France. He was called John Lamb, but we will call him John ap Lamb or Ieuan Lawgoch.

Danger! Lose a home and enjoy a bun

Not long after the last war was declared, the military authorities decided to build a practice range for tanks in the Epynt mountains in Breconshire. With little warning, families were evacuated from the homes they had lived in for generations. A Welsh-speaking community was destroyed almost overnight. The range is still used and if you go there today to enjoy the magnificent scenery, you might be confronted by a sign, PERYGL (danger) and a flying red flag (baner goch). If you are wise, you will hurry away around Dixie Corner or along the Burma Road, two of the many English place-names introduced to the area.

If we wish to say that something is dangerous in Welsh, we would say, 'Ma fe'n beryglus'. This is the most commonly used form in north Wales, though they will also say, 'Mae o'n beryg'. But you could well hear someone in south Wales ask, 'Ydy e'n ddanjerus?'

The Welsh language borrows many words from the English but this is not an example. A form of the word, 'dansier', was spoken in Wales over four hundred years ago, so use it.

But the word 'haste' (brys) was borrowed, albeit a very long time ago. It is used mainly in south Wales. If you wish to hurry someone along in north Wales, you would say, 'Brysia/Brysiwch!' In south Wales, you might hear, 'Hastia/Hastiwch!' though the lingering might have been due to enjoyment. The Welsh for 'to enjoy' is 'mwynhau'; however many feel (wrongly) that this has a literary flavour; consequently, they have borrowed from the English and say, 'enjoio'. They might even cut off the first two letters and say, 'joio'. If they wish to say that they enjoyed themselves immensely, they will say, 'Joio ma's draw'. This idiom defies translation.

Not so very long ago, the military authorities decided to alleviate their consciences regarding the commandeering of Epynt and arranged a magnificent tea party for the evacuees. It's a pity that all of them did not rush to eat the buns and cakes. Would they have enjoyed themselves? Probably not.

I swear, but so what?

Goronwy Owen, one of the greatest poets of the eighteenth century, was born in Anglesey. He wrote a famous poem called 'Dydd y Farn' (Judgement Day). In it he describes hell as the residence of the devil and his tenants, not a good place in which to live. He was accused once of being one of the devil's tenants himself, spending far too much time on his backside, or bum, in taverns quaffing ale; but to him, working in destitute English parishes was hell and he always pined for his native Anglesey. He died on a cotton plantation in America.

The Welsh word for 'devil' is the comparatively new word, 'diafol', from the Latin, 'diabolus'. Goronwy Owen used the old Welsh word, 'diawl' happily, but today it is frowned upon as a swear word and should not be uttered by genteel people.

The rude Welsh word for 'bum' is 'tin', but it is also an obsolete word for 'tail'. It is more rude to use this by itself than 'diafol'. One of the Welsh words for the English metal, 'tin' is 'tun', always spelt with an 'u'. Spell it with an 'i' and you are the devil's tenant.

But we use 'tin' happily in conjunction with other words. For example, if we wish to say that someone is dawdling, we say, 'Ma' fe'n/hi'n tin-droi' (Turning his/her bum). The Welsh for 'head over heels' is 'tin-dros-ben'. An old Welsh word for 'petticoat' is 'tinbais', by today the initial 'tin' has been dropped. The Welsh for 'the tail of the craft' used to be 'tincerdd'—the 'dd' has been dropped and we have 'tincer', a word to describe a mender of pots and pans.

It is said in a lighter vein that a learner has not crossed the language bridge until he is able to swear in Welsh. These two devilish words should give you a head start, or should I say a tail start?

Walking for the word of God

One of the most romantic journeys in Welsh history was undertaken by a young lady called Mary Jones. She walked barefoot from her home near the village of Abergynolwyn to Bala, a journey of about twenty five miles, so that she could purchase a Welsh bible from Thomas Charles, Bala. She thought initially that hers had been a wasted journey as there were no bibles left for sale. But Thomas Charles took pity on her and gave her his own bible.

One of the Welsh words for 'journey' is the colloquial expression derived from the English 'journey', 'siwrnai'; but what you will probably hear is 'siwrne'. Mary Jones could have informed Thomas Charles, 'Fe ges i siwrne bell'. If you make a fruitless journey, the expression to use is 'siwrne seithug'. Had Mary gone home without her bible, she could have said, 'Fe ges i siwrne seithug i'r Bala'.

But 'siwrnai' has developed another meaning, 'once' in south Wales. You might hear the word used in Welsh rugby commentaries, in a sentence such as, 'Siwrne iddo fe ga'l y bêl, bant ag e'. (Once he had the ball, away he went). If you ask someone who is busy to go for a walk with you, he/she might say, 'Siwrne ifi orffen hwn, fe ddo(f) i'. If you know where you are going, you can say, 'Rwy'n siŵr o'm siwrne'. People euphemistically describe man's last journey from this world to the next as 'Siwrne Dafydd Broffwyd'.

The tale of Mary Jones's barefoot journey has spread across the world, often borne by missionaries. On life's journey, she lived to the ripe old age of 88 and her bible is now in the library of University College, Cambridge. The fact that many young girls at that time were used to walking for many miles without footwear should not be allowed to spoil a good story.

An elusive hero and a disappearing negative

In 1993, the fourth centenary of the death of John Penry, of Cefn-brith, Llangammarch Wells, Powys, the first Welsh Christian martyr, was commemorated. He was a thirty year old father of four daughters when he died in London in 1593. He was not happy with the way the queen appointed non Welsh-speaking bishops to dioceses; he was not happy with the scarcity of Welsh-language bibles and he was not afraid to express his views at a very dangerous time for Puritans. The authorities were not happy with these views and he was executed.

The Welsh for 'not' is 'ni/nid', but it can be a very elusive word before verbs. The general rule is that we use 'nid' before vowels and 'ni' before consonants, for example: 'Nid oedd y plant gartre', or 'Ni chafodd y neges', or 'Ni (g)welais i'r dyn llaeth y bore 'ma'. Note that the rule still operates even if the initial consonant is mutated out of a word. But two of the structures quoted above have a literary flavour and are rarely used in conversation is such a form. What you would hear would be, '(Ni) Does dim amser gen i', or '(Ni) Wela i neb ar y ffordd'.

'Dim' and 'nage' are often substituted (incorrectly) for 'nid' in conversation. A correct structure would be, 'Nid fi adawodd y drws ar agor', and this is often used. But look out for other colloquial forms such as, 'Dim fi fwytodd yr afal', or 'Nage fi wariodd yr arian'. You will know that 'nage' means 'no' or 'not so'. It should not be used in such a construction.

If you wish to visit John Penry's birthplace, that also can be elusive. A few present-day scholars say that he was not born in Cefn-brith and that his roots are really in north Glamorganshire.

(Nage)/Nid fi sy'n dweud. Haneswyr sy'n dweud.

Cefn-brith, cartref John Penry

A tenor with a voice like a nightingale

If you ever go to Dowlais, near Merthyr Tudful, stand by the river Morlais. Its waters are remarkably clean. Had you been able to visit the area well over a century ago, you would not have been able to hear its trickle because of the noise of industry. The orphan Robert Rees would not have been allowed to play in the dirty waters of the Morlais; in any case he was working in the local coal-mine when he was nine. He loved to sing, and he joined the chapel temperance choir. A few years later, his voice had brought him such fame that he was described as 'Tenor Cenedlaethol Cymru' (The National Tenor of Wales).

When you use the conjunction 'os' (if), take care. You will use it in a conditional sentence, such as, 'Os wyt ti'n siarad Cymraeg, da iawn', or, 'Os wyt ti'n mynd allan, gwisga gôt gynnes', or, 'Os wyt ti'n mynd i Ddowlais, dos at afon Morlais'.

. Almost always, the verb follows 'os'. 'Os daw hi'n gynnar, rho de iddi hi'. 'Os gwelwch chi Rita, dywedwch fod te'n barod'. Many, quite incorrectly, place a 'y' before this verb. You should never say, 'Rho arian iddo fe os y daw e'.

It is correct to say, 'Os fi sydd i wneud y te, popeth yn iawn', but people tend to use 'mai' (or 'taw') after 'os' and you will hear, 'Os taw heno mae'r cyngerdd, fedra i ddim dod', or 'Os mai Eos Morlais (Morlais Nightingale) sy'n canu, mae'n rhaid i fi gael tocyn'.

When Robert Rees realised that he could sing like a nightingale, he chose a stage name for himself: Eos Morlais, and as Eos Morlais, he sang 'Hen Wlad fy Nhadau' with the eisteddfod choir at the National Eisteddfod in Bangor, helping it to become our national anthem. History records that his singing of the song 'took the eisteddfod by storm' (see page 15).

If you would like to get away from it all

If you travel north from Pontrhydfendigaid in Ceredigion and proceed on the mountain road through the village of Ffair-rhos you will eventually arrive at a bleak and wild hinterland. If you climb to the highest vantage point you will arrive at a flat-topped boulder. If you climb this boulder which is called Carreg Nawllyn (nine lake stone) you will be able to see nine lakes, the five Teifi lakes plus three nearby lakes and the uppermost reaches of the Claerwen dam. The view is well worth the journey.

I have mentioned on page 134 that you must be very careful with 'os', the Welsh for 'if'. You often come across it in a conditional clause, for example, 'Os oes amser gennych chi, dewch draw heno', but if you reply, 'Dw i ddim yn siŵr os oes amser gen i', you are committing an error. The correct sentence is, 'Dw i ddim yn siŵr a oes amser gen i' ('a' instead of 'os'). This error possibly occurs because the speaker thinks of the English 'whether/if', translating this as 'os'. Examples of defective sentences that you might hear are, 'Dw i ddim yn gwybod os bydd hi'n dod' (. . . a fydd hi'n dod), or, 'Tybed os oes amser gen ti?' (. . . a oes amser gen ti?)

'Os' is also used in an idiomatically flavoured statement, if you wish to emphasise a point. You can say, 'Heb os nac oni bai', in certain situations. This translates roughly as, 'Without an "if" or a "but for"'; for example, in a command, 'Heb os nac oni bai, fe fyddi di yma erbyn chwech o'r gloch'.

Had you climbed Carreg Nawllyn shortly before the Claerwen dam was opened, you would only have seen eight lakes, as one nearby lake has dried up over the years. But now there are nine again as everything comes to him who waits.

Going for a ride on different buses

The first buses were introduced as far back as 1662. The first petrol driven motor bus was introduced in Germany in 1895. It could seat eight passengers inside and two others outside on the driver's box. The first motorised bus service in Britain was introduced in Bradford in 1897. It charged a fare of two pennies for a two mile journey.

You will be aware in conversation that the Welsh word for 'bus' is usually 'bys'. However, if you look on the sides of buses you will often see the word 'bws'. That is what you will find in dictionaries. This form has been slow to establish itself.

If you say, 'Rhaid i fi ddal y bws', you will be in a minority, but if you write, 'Roedd y bys yn llawn', you are confronted by another problem as 'bys' (with the clear, long sound) is the Welsh for 'finger'. Writers who prefer to write 'bỳs' for the vehicle often place an accent on the 'y' to show that it is obscure and short.

You are offered a choice of plurals, the commonly used 'bysys' and a Welsh form, 'bysiau'. You will see the latter in print but people usually say 'bysys'.

Pay attention to the plural form and do not write 'bysus'. Note that 'rasys' is the plural of 'ras'. This conforms to a pattern with 'bocs— bocsys', 'nyrs—nyrsys'. A popular S4C television programme on trotting races some time ago was incorrectly titled 'Rasus'. This is a common error and you can have 'matsus' instead of 'matsys' and 'letus' instead of 'letys'. As such errors occur often on the media they could well supersede the correct form that might die out.

Meanwhile, until it dies, always travel in the bus and not on the bus, and if you are writing in Welsh that you have to catch buses, do so with a 'y', and remember that the last horse-drawn bus in Britain ceased running in 1932 when one of the horses died.

Let pain be a warning always

Many scholars will tell you that King Arthur never existed, but we know differently. I mentioned on page 75 that he is still alive. Tradition/folklore tells us that he was wounded in the Battle of Camlan and that his faithful knight Bedwyr threw his sword Excalibur (Caledfwlch) into a magical lake near the battlefield. Before it touched the waters, a hand rose from the water to grab the hilt. Bedwyr then carried his king to the edge of this lake where a ship was waiting to take him to the Isle of Avalon (Afallon), an isle where there is no pain and suffering.

Expressing 'pain and suffering' can be a problem for learners. I mentioned 'cur pen' (headache) or 'dant tost' (painful tooth) on page 102. I also mentioned, 'Mae fy mys i'n gwnio' (My finger is aching). If someone has a headache in parts of north Wales, he/she might say, 'Mae (fy) mhen i'n brifo'. This expression is also used in other parts of Wales. You will probably be familiar with the first line of Llanelli's local anthem: 'Mae bys Meri Ann wedi brifo'. Had the rhyme not been the relevant factor here, the people of Llanelli might have been happier saying, 'Mae bys Meri Ann wedi 'nafu' (anafu = to hurt).

They might have said also, 'Mae hi wedi cael lo(e)s', the full expression here being 'loes'. The plural form, 'loesau', is hardly ever used. Another word for pain is 'poen'. Again, what you might hear is 'pôn' the 'e' often being dropped in conversation. The often used plural form, 'poenau', is eroded to 'poene' in conversation, and we might hear, 'Ma' fe mewn poene, druan bach!'

Arthur was a wise king, and he must have fervently hoped that he could introduce pain to Avalon, as it is a warning that things might not be as they should in the human body.

A fishy tale of fish and chips

One nursery rhyme from the seventh century is called 'Pais Dinogad' (Dinogad's petticoat). In it Dinogad promises her young ones that their father would catch fish by Derwennydd waterfall (rhaeadr). This would provide them with an adequate supper. The monasteries of that time also included plenty of fish in their fare. Much later in time, Giraldus Cambrensis praised the salmon rivers of Teifi, Dee, Usk and Wye. Llangorse lake was rich in tench, pike and trout; perch and eels were plentiful in the lakes of Snowdonia. Fish is not so plentiful in our rivers and lakes these days, but we are still fond of our fish and chips.

The Welsh for 'fish' is 'pysgodyn', plural 'pysgod'. Catching fish is 'pysgota', but when they buy the commodity, most Welsh-language speakers use the English word, 'fish'.

If you would like to order a rainbow trout in a restaurant, ask for 'brithyll yr enfys'. 'A piece of salmon', would be 'darn o eog', but most people say 'samwn', an acceptable word that is recorded in dictionaries. The fish that is usually eaten with chipped potatoes is cod, but as the word 'cod' has a Welsh flavour, people rarely use the indigenous word, 'penfras'. You can order fish and chips in Welsh. Just ask for 'py(sgod) a sglod(ion)'. 'Sgod a sglod' trip easily off the tongue.

Many years ago, a staple fish amongst the poor was the salted herring. The Welsh for 'herring' in south Wales is 'ysgadenyn', but people usually drop the 'y' in the singular and the plural which is '(y)sgadan'. If you wish to buy herring in north Wales, ask for a 'penwaig' or a 'pennog'. One fish, the 'gwyniad' is found only in Bala lake but because it swims deep it is rarely caught. Don't confuse this with 'gwyniad y môr', 'whiting'.

If you cannot remember a particular Welsh word for a species of fish, just think of it as the one that got away.

Good shepherds prefer guarding cows

I have mentioned previously that transhumance was practised in Wales up to a few years ago. I described how cattle would be driven up from the 'hendre' (winter abode) to the 'hafod' (summer abode). This allowed grass (glaswellt) to grow on the valley floors so that it could be harvested as hay (gwair) for winter fodder. During this time the word 'bugail' meant 'cowherd'. His task was to guard the cows/cattle in the 'hafod'.

The prefix 'bu' (meaning 'cows') appears in a few words in Welsh. There is 'buarth' (cow yard/farmyard) for example, but the word can be used in other contexts. In south Wales schools, children play on the 'maes chwar(a)e' (playground) but in north Wales they play on the 'buarth'.

You will know that the Welsh for 'cow' is 'buwch'. In north Wales they refer to a herd of cows as 'buches' and you could hear, 'Mae'r fuches yn mynd i'r beudy' (see page 32).

The collective word for 'cattle' is 'gwartheg' but I have mentioned previously that cattle (and cows) are often referred to as 'da' in south Wales. Someone might say, 'Rwy'n mynd i'r cae i nôl y da nawr'. 'Milking cows' would be 'da godro', but you could also hear 'gwartheg godro'. 'Da' is referred to in the parable of the prodigal son in the bible as 'goods', but this meaning has fallen into disuse.

Today when we say 'bugail' we mean a shepherd, but orally, what you would hear would be 'bugel'. In the realms of the scriptures, 'the good shepherd' is referred to in Welsh as 'y bugail da'. There is a historical double meaning here, as the shepherd was a 'bugail "da"' before he ever was a 'bugail defaid'.

A quick cuddle can work wonders

One Welsh name for 'hare' is 'oen (lamb) bach Melangell'. According to legend the prince of Powys and his hounds were coursing a hare across moorland in north Powys. They came upon it in a grassy clearing, being cuddled by a maiden who introduced herself as Melangell, the daughter of the king of Ireland. She explained that she had come to Wales as her tyrant of a father wished her to marry someone she did not love and that God had led her to this spot. The terrified hounds would not venture near them and fled in confusion. The huntsman realised that God had given Melangell power to protect the weak and offered her the clearing to be a sanctuary for wild animals.

A commonly used word for a cuddle in south Wales is 'cwtsh', a word not found in dictionaries. A mother might say, 'Ma'r babi'n lico cwtsh bach cyn mynd i gysgu'. A wife might tell her husband, 'Gad i fi gwtsho miwn' (Let me cuddle in). It most probably derives from the English, 'couch', a word of many meanings.

It is not a commonly used expression in north Wales. There they might prefer to say, 'Rwy'n hoffi rhoi maldod i'r gath', or, 'Ma'r babi'n hoffi mwytha(u)'.

But it has other meanings in Welsh as well. The Welsh for 'hole under the stairs' in south Wales is 'cwtsh dan stâr'. It is traditionally the home of the hobgoblin (called 'bwci bo') that refractory children are occasionally threatened with. A mother might say, 'Fe ddaw'r bwci bo ar d'ôl di'. In north Wales he resides in the 'twll dan grisie' or 'sbens' and is called 'bwgan'. A common idiom for raising false fears is 'codi bwganod' in a sentence such as, 'Paid â chodi bwganod, da thi'.

'Cwtsh' (again derived from 'couch') is used to describe the coarse grasses in lawns. As a verb noun form, it is used with an appended 'o' to describe 'crouching'. A command in school might be, 'Cwtshwch lawr i gyd, blant'.

Melangell could well have been crouching in the coarse grass to offer 'cwtsh' to the frightened hare, a most effective way of calming the rapidly beating heart.

Eglwys Pennant Melangell yng ngogledd Powys

A time and a place for confusion

According to legend, Llywelyn the Great ordered his dog, Gelert, to guard his cradled, sleeping child whilst he was away hunting for a few hours. The faithful hound obeyed his master and when a wolf (blaidd) entered the place where the cradle was kept, Gelert killed it. When Llywelyn returned he saw the upturned cradle and a very bloodied Gelert. He immediately slew the dog. Presently he heard a whimpering noise and discovered that his child was alive and well under the upturned cradle and by the dead wolf.

One Welsh word for 'place' is 'man'. The Welsh for 'presently' is 'yn y man' (not 'yn y fan'—there is no mutation). With reference to 'place', you could say, 'Mae bedd Gelert yn y fan hon' (feminine) or . . . yn y man hwn' (masculine), both expressions being correct. A popular idiom to describe a specific location is 'yn y fan a'r lle', for example, 'Rown i yn y fan a'r lle (I was there) pan weles i'r blaidd'. If you say, 'Fe fydda i gyda thi yn y man', you are saying that you will be with a certain person presently. We can say of the greener grass that a person might see in his neighbours's field, 'Man gwyn, man draw' (roughly translated, A white place, a distant place). There is no mutation.

If the 'a' in 'man' is circumflexed, it means 'small' or 'fine'; 'hadau mân' for example, means 'small' or 'fine seeds'. Finally, you might hear a person say, 'Man a man i fi fynd'. 'Man + man' has nothing to do with either time or place. It means, I might as well go.

If you feel like shedding a tear for Gelert, remember that a similar tale is popular in India. There, a guardian mongoose dispatched an invading snake . A case of a tale depending on the place.

Never on Tuesday but often on Sunday

On 26 March (Mawrth) 1851, Robert Ambrose Jones was born in Abergele. He is better known by his pen name, Emrys ap Iwan. He was a fluent linguist and a vitriolic writer. He was a staunch fighter against what was known in his day in Wales as the English Cause. Prominent Welsh Presbyterians arranged to build English-language chapels in the heartland of Welsh communities so that the souls of the English people who had settled there might be saved (via these chapels). Many such chapels were built in Wales. Because of his writings, Emrys ap Iwan, a Presbyterian minister, found it very difficult to secure a calling. In those days, it required a brave man to fight against the establishment.

'Mis Mawrth' can cause a problem to learners as 'Mawrth' is also the name of the third day of the week, 'dydd Mawrth'. Most of the Welsh days of the week are also the names of planets: Mawrth (Mars); Mercher (Mercury); Iau (Jupiter); Gwener (Venus); Sadwrn (Saturn). When we refer to the month of March, we would almost always precede it with the Welsh word for 'month' (mis), and we would have 'mis Mawrth'.

This is almost always the method used when we refer to days, and we have 'dydd Mawrth, dydd Mercher', etc . . . The two exceptions are the first and last days of the week. You might hear, 'Rwy'n mynd i'r capel Saesneg ar y Sul', or 'Wyt ti'n mynd i'r gêm ar y Sadwrn?' You will not often hear, 'Rwy'n mynd i siopa ar y Mawrth/Mercher/Iau/Gwener', but you can sometimes hear, '. . . ar y Llun'. Names of days are not always translated (as the dates often are) in a Welsh sentence, i.e., 'Ar ddydd Mawrth y fifteenth y mae fy mhen blwydd i'.

Emrys ap Iwan said, 'Os bydd yr iaith farw, bydd farw yn nhŷ ei chyfeillion' (If the Welsh language dies, it will do so in the house of its friends). The congregations of the English Cause chapels were often mainly composed of Welsh-language speakers. Indeed, it became fashionable to be members in such chapels, so Emrys ap Iwan had a valid point.

When things are just as bad, beware of mortality

There is a highland cemetery between Rhymney and Tredegar; just a scatter of time-worn, unfenced gravestones on the bleak hillside. Many have fallen down; the inscriptions are difficult to read; a few are in Welsh. It is called the cholera cemetery and reminds us of the cholera epidemic that swept through Wales in 1849. 203 people perished in Tredegar alone. Things were as bad in Aberystwyth where 223 perished. 245 died in Neath. Things were not as bad in Newtown; only six people were buried there.

The Welsh equative adjective for 'as bad' is 'cynddrwg' which derives from 'drwg' (bad). It can also mean 'naughty'. It is an irregular adjective, the comparative form being 'gwaeth', and the superlative form, 'gwaethaf'. There are about ten adjectives that do not conform to the rules and must be learnt parrot fashion.

But Welsh speakers can confuse the learner by introducing other forms, particularly with equative adjectives. Usually, equative adjectives of more than one syllable are preceded by 'mor'. You may hear, 'mor hapus', or 'mor ofalus', but 'mor' can appear also before a monosyllabic equative adjective and you might hear, 'Roedd pethe mor ddrwg yn Aberystwyth' (instead of the more usual 'cynddrwg'). Indeed, learners are often advised to ignore the irregularities and use 'mor' (mor fach, mor dda) at all times, but they may well encounter the other forms in conversation and must be aware of them.

There is a tendency for Welsh speakers to compose incorrect forms; for example, you might well hear 'cyn waethed' in a sentence such as, 'Roedd yr eira cyn waethed yng Nghaerdydd ag ym Mangor', or 'Mae merched cyn waethed â bechgyn'.

Misuse can cause problems in English as well. In some parts of Wales, 'bad' can mean 'ill'. One schoolboy, when asked to offer the degrees of 'bad' in an examination wrote, 'Bad, very ill, dead'.

Asking the time of day in a way

One of the oldest practising clock makers of Wales was John Owen of Llanrwst, a gentleman from the Conwy valley. He was working in the town around 1745 and lived by Llanrwst square. At this time it was customary for the sons of gentlemen to become clock makers as clock making was one of the most respectable crafts in the eighteenth century. He was expert at designing and building long case clocks which we refer to as grandfather clocks. He was able to build intricate eight-day ones that were wound by a key and were highly prized.

One of the first Welsh phrases that you might learn is the question, 'Beth ydy'r amser?' (Be' dy'r amser?). This is a translation from the English, 'What is the time?' but in Welsh you will often come across a time query which does not seem to bear any relationship to clocks, 'Faint o'r gloch ydy hi?' This of course follows the phrases, 'saith o'r gloch, wyth o'r gloch', etc. But in one sense, the relationship is tenuous as it can also suggest that a person knows (metaphorically) which way the wind is blowing. You might hear a person who suspects something say, 'Rwy'n gwybod faint ydy hi o'r gloch'.

We also use a translation of the English phrase, 'That rings a bell', = 'Mae hwnna'n canu cloch'. If a person raises his voice, we might warn him, 'Paid codi dy gloch'. This could relate to the Welsh for a cock crow (clochdar), and you could hear a remonstrance 'Paid â chlochdar, was' ('gwas' meaning 'son' or 'boy').

The most familiar bell that we have in Wales is the church bell, referred to as 'cloch y llan' ('llan' here meaning 'church'). We say that a person who has died has been called to his long resting place by 'cloch y llan'. John Owen was called by this bell in 1776, but he has left us priceless legacies that tick away as accurately as they did two centuries ago.

Similarities and probabilities to be aware of

One of our most enduring folk tales tells us about the fairy maid of Llyn y Fan Fach in Carmarthenshire. Rhiwallon, a local shepherd, saw her combing her hair by the lake and fell in love with her. He asked her father for her hand in marriage, but the wily father brought two similar sisters from the lake for him to choose from. He chose correctly, but the subsequent marriage was conditional. Rhiwallon was not to touch her with an iron object more than twice. He failed to adhere to the conditions and the fairy maid returned to the lake, leaving her children behind. They later became famous as 'Meddygon Myddfai' (The Physicians of Myddfai).

'Tebyg' (similar) is a useful word in Welsh. Simply, you could just say, 'Roedd y ddwy ferch yn debyg i'w gilydd', but the word can also mean 'likely'. In response to a question requiring an affirmative reply, you might say, 'Ie, mae'n debyg'. But we often dispense with unnecessary words in conversation, and what you might hear is, 'Ie, (mae'n) debyg'.

The Welsh for likeness, similarity is 'tebygrwydd'. You could say, 'Doedd dim tebygrwydd rhwng y ddwy ferch'. But do not confuse this word with 'tebygolrwydd' which means 'likelihood, probability'. You could say, 'Y tebygolrwydd yw y byddan nhw'n priodi'.

A word which you could confuse with 'tebyg' is 'tebygol' (likely, probable), but if you do, no harm is done, for example, you could say, 'Mae'n debyg o fod yn hwyr', or, 'Mae'n debygol o fod yn hwyr'. The choice is yours, but purists always separate the two meanings.

Poor Rhiwallon had a difficult choice when confronted by two similar girls. But the wily one he had set his heart upon moved her foot forward slightly when he was trying to decide. The probability is that she did this on purpose, but it did the trick!

146

Try printing sheep to solve a problem

I mentioned on page 88 that drovers would have been a familiar sight in rural Wales in the eighteenth century. In the summer and early autumn months they would drive their cattle across the country to cattle fairs in England. I mentioned that they established their own banks. They printed their own bank notes and as these would have been used mainly by illiterate farmers, they designed pictorial ones. The Aberystwyth and Tregaron Bank (Bank y Ddafad Ddu) printed two sheep on its £2 note, one sheep on its £1 note and a lamb on its 10 shilling note; but when they are illustrated in historical publications we are not told what was printed on the other side of the notes.

Be wary of 'of the'. It is easy for the learner to be influenced by the English and say 'o' instead of 'i' when translating in his mind a phrase such as, 'the other side of the town' into Welsh. He might well say, incorrectly, 'yr ochor arall o'r (of the) dref'. The correct Welsh expression is, 'yr ochor arall i'r dref'. Similarly, you should say, 'tu allan i'r siop', and not 'tu allan o'r siop'.

If you wish to say that someone is a friend of the family, you should say, 'Cyfaill i'r teulu ydy e' (not 'o'r'). On the same basis, this sentence is incorrect, 'O ganlyniad o godi'n hwyr, fe gollais i'r trên'. The sentence should commence, 'O ganlyniad i . . .'

Finally, if you translate a sentence such as, 'The tendency not to carry too much money', you should commence with, 'Y duedd i beidio . . .' (not 'o beidio . . .')

As the developing trains shunted the drovers to an economic decline, they had a tendency to print too many notes without gold to back them. This proved to be their downfall, but governments still follow their example.

Some things don't come to the one who waits

One of our most poignant tales is set in Nant Gwrtheyrn, the popular Language Centre. Many years ago, on the morning of her wedding, Meinir, following custom, ran in her wedding dress from the house to hide from Rhys, her sweetheart. After a few minutes he went to look for her. He and friends scoured the countryside but she could not be seen anywhere. He waited for her at the altar in the local church hoping that she would make an appearance. But she did not. Then one day, many years hence, lightning struck a hollow oak tree by her home. It split open, revealing a skeleton in the remains of a wedding dress.

I have mentioned previously that one Welsh word for 'to wait' is 'disgwyl'. But 'aros' can mean the same thing. You could hear, 'Fe arhoses (or 'Fe ddisgwylies i') i amdanat ti am orie (hours)'. If someone asks you to wait for him, he could say, 'Aros amdana i', the correct grammatical form, or 'Rhosa amdana i', the word 'rhosa' being a colloquial expression. The Welsh for 'Waiting Room' is 'Ystafell Aros'.

But 'disgwyl' can refer to pregnancy. If someone tells you, 'Mae Meinir yn disgwyl', it means that Meinir is expecting a child, the word 'plentyn/babi' (child/baby) having been omitted from the end of the sentence.

Many Welsh speakers do not seem to be happy with 'aros' or 'disgwyl' for 'to wait'. They prefer instead to offer a rough translation of the English, 'to wait', and you could hear, 'Fe fydda i'n weitiad amdanat ti'. This is a corrupt oral expression and you should not come across it in a written form.

Never wait for your sweetheart under a tree in a thunderstorm. Wait long enough, and lightning might well strike it. Rhys waited for years before lightning struck the Nant Gwrtheyrn tree.

Pentref Nant Gwrtheyrn

Truly love being Welsh in Welsh, please

I mentioned on page 21 that the Britons of 'Wales' many centuries ago expressed a desire to be described as 'Cymry' the plural of 'Cymro', a compound of 'com', a prefix meaning 'together' and 'bro' meaning 'border, coast' or 'district'. But it is almost impossible to say when these 'Cymry' developed a sense of nationality. The general belief is that this consciousness emerged in most people around the thirteenth century, but the picture was clouded somewhat from 1066 onwards when many Normans settled in Wales. There were many who fought the new enemy but there were others who became collaborators.

This was brought to mind recently when I chanced upon a big circular, colourful lapel badge produced to be sold in tourist offices; an excellent idea. It bore the slogan, 'Rwy'n falch i fod yn Gymro'. This sentiment is marred somewhat by the fact that the sentence is influenced by the English, and more especially by the preposition 'to'. Here, 'I'm glad to be . . .' has given birth to the 'Rwy'n falch i fod . . .' It is more correct to say, 'Rwy'n falch bod yn Gymro'. The 'i' is superfluous.

Similarly, a remark such as 'Rwy'n hoffi/Dwy i ddim yn hoffi i yfed cwrw', should be, 'Rwy'n hoffi/Dw i ddim yn hoffi yfed gwin', again without the preposition.

Many say, incorrectly, 'Dywedais i'r plant', instead of 'Dywedais wrth y plant'. Here, there is a temptation to use 'i' after the verb. You should ask, 'Gwna gymwynas (favour) â mi', and not 'Gwna gymwynas i fi'. Similarly you should say, 'Rhennir y llyfr yn bedair rhan', and not 'Rhennir y llyfr i bedair rhan'.

Indeed, as you master the language you might like to construct a colourful badge with the slogan 'Rwy'n hoffi siarad Cymraeg cywir' on it. Respect its longevity.

Guests can be confused in some hotels

Historians remind us that Florence Nightingale was a famous benefactress. When she was 34 years old she went with thirty other nurses to work in Scutari hospital in the Crimea and raised standards of cleanliness and care there. She was also instrumental in helping to establish the first ever hospital staffed by trained nurses in 1855. But the other nurses who worked in the Crimea with her are hardly ever mentioned. One of them, Beti (or Betsi) Cadwaladr, came from Bala. She was not a trained hospital nurse but she did sterling work there.

Many Welsh speakers ignore the familiar Welsh word for 'ysbyty' and offer sentences such as, 'Rwy'n mynd i'r hospital fory'. But you will find that those who use 'ysbyty' will sometimes use the feminine gender and sometimes the masculine gender. They might say, 'Mae ysbyty fawr yng Nghaerdydd', and 'Dwy i ddim yn hoffi'r ysbyty hwn'. The correct form is 'ysbyty hwn'. Treat 'hospital' as masculine always.

At one time you had a choice of two plural forms, 'ysbytyau' and 'ysbytai', but the former (more correct) form has become obsolete.

Another word for a type of building which can cause problems is 'gwesty'. Some people use it as a translation of 'hotel', ignoring the English word. Some prefer 'hotel' as it causes less confusion. Others favour 'gwesty' as the Welsh for 'guest house', but this can cause confusion when the guest and the building come together in a sentence. A common plural form for 'gwesty' is 'gwestyau'. Another acceptable form is 'gwestai', but this plural form can also mean 'guest', and when you say that the guests went into all the hotels, what you have is, 'Fe aeth y gwestai i'r gwestai i gyd'. Bearing this in mind, it is better to use 'gwestyau' for hotels and guest houses and 'gwestai' for 'guest'.

The first ever hotel was opened in London by David Low in 1774. His venture was not a success and he became a chiropodist instead.

Turkeys see nothing to be pleased about in celebrations

Most people are pleased when they have turkey for dinner. The bird was brought to Europe from America in the sixteenth century. It was very common there and was often eaten by the first settlers in commemorative landing feasts. At one time, everything that came from the Middle East was associated with Turkey. Many thought that the turkey had come from Turkey and it was unfortunately given a misleading name. It is still the most popular commemorative edible bird and well over six million offer pleasant eating with cranberry sauce every year in Britain.

The Welsh for 'please' is 'os gwelwch chi'n dda', but most people say 'plîs' quite readily in a phrase such as, 'Rhagor o de, plîs', as the word is quite acceptable in conversation. But many are reluctant to write 'plîs', especially in an official capacity, and this can initiate queries when bilingual forms and signs are produced. 'Please sign below', for example, should be 'Arwyddwch isod, os gwelwch chi'n dda'. Unfortunately, most form boxes requiring a 'please' are designed to accommodate the length of the English wordage and there is often no room for the longer Welsh phrase.

Sometimes, another expression, 'Byddwch cystal ag . . .' (Be as good as to . . .) is used instead. Some mutate 'cystal' and you will read, 'Byddwch gystal . . .' However, this does not solve the problem of space.

'Please' is a shortened and acceptable form of, 'If it pleases you', but it is not possible to shorten 'os gwelwch chi'n dda', satisfactorily, with the result that the courtesy phrase is often omitted in translations. This gives the impression that one does not wish to be courteous in Welsh.

Commemorating became so popular in America at one time that the turkey was nearly wiped out and had to be protected. Nobody was pleased about this, apart from the poor turkey, that is.

Mutations can cause vegetables to rot

The first Prince of Wales, the son of King Edward I, was elevated in 1301. Centuries later, in 1584, the story that he was presented to Wales at that time as a child prince was recorded. It stated that the king had promised that the child would not be able to speak English, thus duping the Welsh into believing that he would be a Welsh speaker. The story is probably fiction but the present Prince of Wales also has problems with his Welsh. At one time he said wryly that the mutations seem to be a language within a language and in many ways he was speaking the truth.

I have mentioned previously that mutations can sometimes be ignored, and a few are nowadays, but there are important times when mutating (or not mutating) can alter the meaning of a sentence.

Prince Charles does not have a residence in Wales; he prefers to grow vegetables organically on his farm in Gloucestershire (Sir Gaerloyw). Should he wish to open a vegetable shop there, he could have a sign painted which states: SIOP LYSIAU. But if he wished to emphasise that the vegetables were organically grown, he would have to adjust the sign somewhat and paint: SIOP LLYSIAU ORGANIG, ignoring the mutation. If you asked him why, he could tell you that an adjective is mutated after a singular feminine noun, for example, 'cath fach', but when a noun follows another noun there is a genitive relationship between the two and the second noun does not mutate.

But this is a very grey area in Welsh. If the prince wished to post a letter he might well go to a Post Office (Swyddfa'r Post), the correct form, but many might say, in conversation, 'Dw i'n mynd i'r swyddfa bost'.

If the prince had made the mistake of calling a health food shop, SIOP FWYDYDD IACH (with the mutation) he would have implied that the food was not unhealthy or rotting. The correct expression should have been: SIOP BWYDYDD IACH. Long live the veg!

153

Death can come in various ways, even to horses

Historians say that the most important person buried in Llanycil cemetery near Bala is Thomas Charles. I have mentioned him before on page 131. He was the main force behind the ordination of Presbyterian ministers so that Presbyterianism could continue to flourish in Wales. He fell in a faint off his horse on Sunday night, 24 July 1814. He died at the beginning of October, and his wife, a prominent Bala shopkeeper, died three weeks after him. There is no record of when the horse passed away, but technically, in Welsh, it did not die.

If you wish to say in Welsh that someone died yesterday, you would say, 'Bu e farw ddoe', or 'Fe fu e farw ddoe'. You might well hear, 'Buodd e farw ddoe', but you should not say, incorrectly, 'Fe farwodd e ddoe', though such a statement is gaining in popularity orally.

If you feel that a particular day is rather dull and heavy, you can say, 'Mae hi'n farwedd (farwaidd) iawn heddiw'. If a piece of wood is smouldering, in some parts of Wales you might hear someone say, 'Ma fe'n marw-losgi', but in other parts you might hear instead, 'Ma fe'n mud-losgi' (burning mutely).

I implied that Thomas Charles' horse did not 'die' as in Welsh only people die. When an animal has died we say, 'Ma fe wedi trigo'. If it died yesterday, we would say, 'Fe drigodd e ddoe'. But it is just as correct to say, 'Roedd Thomas Charles yn trigo gyda'i wraig mewn siop yn y Bala', as 'trigo' can also mean 'to dwell/abide'.

A prominent historian saw a child in Llanycil cemetery one day and he said, 'Name the most important person who is buried in this cemetery'. With a tear in his eye, the child answered, 'My mother, sir'.

If only spiders could sing

One problem that has been confronting the National Eisteddfod in recent times is the dearth of competing choirs. Excuses offered are, 'No time to learn the pieces', or 'The high cost of transport'. Were Griffith Rhys Jones (known as Caradog), from Aberdare, alive he would be most surprised. On 10 July 1872 his mixed choir of 456 voices, drawn from all over south Wales, went to the Crystal Palace in London to compete. They had to rehearse eight separate pieces, one of which being for six voices. Competing against them was the London Choir under the baton of Joseph Proudman, but the prize went to 'côr Caradog'. There is a statue to Caradog with his baton in his hand on Aberdare Square. It was carved by Syr William Goscombe John (1860-1952), a famous Welsh sculptor who was born in Cardiff (see page 110).

'Côr' is a word of more than one meaning in Welsh. If you say, 'Dw i'n canu yn y côr', you could be saying that you have joined a choir but you could also be saying that you were singing in a chapel pew, 'côr' being a Welsh word for 'pew'. When a farmer feeds his cows in his cow shed, the animals would be standing in the 'côr' (stall).

But word erosion could present you with still another problem. In south Wales, a spider is referred to as 'corryn' and its web is referred to as 'cwyr cor' (both words without a circumflex), but many refer to it colloquially as 'cwyr côr', with a circumflex. This pronunciation is incorrect, but 'cor' (again without a circumflex) can also mean a tiny person. This is hardly ever used, but you will be aware of 'corgi' (small dog). A name for a very small person is 'corrach'.

They do not have this problem in north Wales. There they refer to a spider as a 'pry cop' and a spider's web as 'gwe pry cop'. But beware! 'pry cop' can never be a translation of 'chief constable'.

A castle too many, thought Alice in wonder

When Edward I commenced building Beaumaris castle in 1295, his aim was to strengthen his defence of the Menai Straits (afon Menai) and keep the Welsh in check. But the castle proved to be something of an anticlimax. Its formidable defences were never tested. There were hardly any significant events in its history until the Civil War when it was held by the Royalists until 1646. When his force was threatened, one royalist officer locked his men up in the church tower and fled, earning for himself the nickname of Captain Church.

The word 'pan' (when) in Welsh should never be followed by 'y mae', nor should it be followed by 'y' or 'yn'. It is incorrect to say, 'Rho de iddo fe pan y daw'. You should say, for example, 'Pan ddaw i'r tŷ, rho groeso iddo fe'.

It is not strictly correct to say, 'Pan mae e'n sâl, mae'n crio'. You should say, 'Pan fo'n sâl, mae'n mynd i'r gwely'. This rule is sometimes ignored and people say, 'Pan mae e'n hapus mae e'n gwenu'.

Other correct form are, 'Pan fydda i yn y dre, fe fydda i'n galw', or 'Pan oedd Lewis Carroll ym Miwmares, fe aeth i weld y castell', or 'Gorffennodd ei waith cartre pan oedd y newyddion yn dechre'.

Many say, 'Pan yn y dre, cofiwch alw'. This is incorrect. You should say, 'Pan fyddwch yn y dre, ewch i'r amgueddfa newydd'. Simply, 'pan' is followed by the verb in an affirmative clause. In a negative clause, 'na' follows 'pan', for example, 'Pan na weles i Siwsan, es i adre', or, 'Pan na fydd arian gen i, rwy'n aros gartre'.

Beaumaris castle has many underground passages. Critics think that when Lewis Carrol walked through them, ideas for tales about Alice in the wonderland came to his mind.

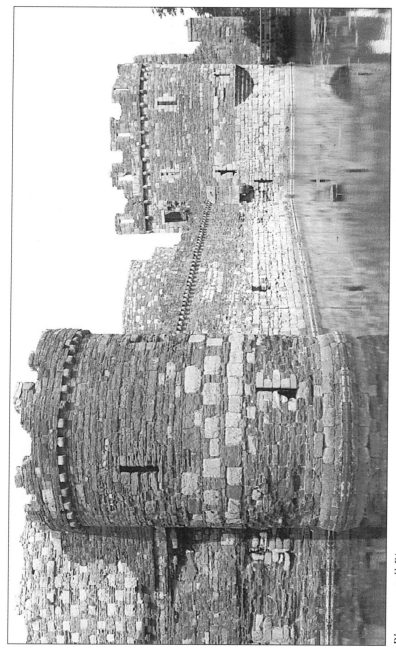

Rhan o gastell Biwmares

Making a meal out of fasting, unfortunately

An unsolved mystery in south Ceredigion is that of Sarah Jacob, the 'Welsh Fasting Girl', the title of a book written about her in 1904. In 1867, when she was ten years old, Sarah unfortunately began starving herself. For two years she was reputed not to have eaten a morsel or drunk a drop of water, and though she was confined to bed she looked remarkably healthy and the local doctor and vicar attributed her condition to divine intervention. Her family did well from her starvation and they charged people who came in their hundreds to witness what unfortunately appeared to be a miracle.

We have more than one word in Welsh for 'unfortunately'. The most common word is 'anffodus', and you could hear, 'Yn anffodus, fe gollodd y bechgyn eu gêm yn erbyn yr ysgol newydd'. Another way of expressing 'alas' would be 'gwaetha'r modd', in a sentence such as, 'Gwaetha'r modd, roedd y car yn mynd yn rhy gyflym'. 'Gwaetha'r modd' translates as 'worse luck' and has a slight slangy flavour. 'Gwaetha(f)' is the superlative form of the adjective 'drwg' and 'modd' is 'means'. You could use an opposite expression, 'gorau'r modd', but as we rarely seem to be happy, it is hardly ever used.

You might well hear an expression which wears a more scholarly flavour, 'ysywaeth'. It is often used on the Welsh news. *Y Geiriadur Mawr* translates this expression as 'more's the pity' and you could hear it in a sentence such as, 'Ysywaeth, does dim llawer o lyfrau Cymraeg i ddysgwyr'.

Beware when you hear this expression as a few speakers use it incorrectly and you could hear, 'Ysywaeth, mae rhagor o lyfrau Cymraeg i ddysgwyr yn cael eu cyhoeddi'. Here the word has a directly opposite meaning, but unfortunately it never means 'fortunately'.

You could hear it in response to a query such as, 'Fyddi di yn y gêm dydd Sadwrn?' 'Na fydda, ysywaeth'.

After two years of observing Sarah Jacob four nurses were brought from Guy's Hospital, London, to oversee her in her bed. Unfortunately, she died after a fortnight of their vigilance, but her mother still maintained, 'Tawn i'n llwgu, 'chafodd hi ddim bwyd', and people are still asking, 'Was this a miracle?'

Nearly there, but not quite

May 29, 1953, was the day when Sir Edmund Hilary from New Zealand and Sherpa Tenzing from Nepal stood on the summit of Mount Everest, probably the first people to do so. Their feat was much acclaimed in Britain. But 33 year old Charles Evans F.R.C.S., a Welshman, a member of the expedition, and a surgeon at Walton Hospital, Liverpool, must have been rather frustrated, because, had circumstances been right, he would have been the first to climb higher than anybody else in the world. In other words, he nearly made it. But he did climb quite as high in the academic world. He became principal of the University of North Wales at Bangor although there were those who felt that he could well have done more to promote the Welsh language and its culture whilst he was in office.

Being nearly there is frustrating and this is what often happens when learners use the word for 'nearly' which is 'bron'. You might hear the correct sentence, 'Mae'r cinio bron â bod yn barod', but people more often than not drop the relative pronoun 'â' in conversation and it is often dropped in written sentences as well.

It can cause problems with mutations, but that statement is only nearly right. If you say, 'Roedd bron bawb yn y dosbarth heno', you will be incorrect. There is no need to mutate 'pawb', the subject of the sentence. The correct expression is, 'Mae bron pawb wedi dysgu'r gwaith'. (You might well encounter 'ymron' instead of 'bron', but both mean 'nearly/almost' and are interchangeable.)

Remember also that you never have 'bron' followed by 'yn' after the verb noun. Never say, 'Mae'r plant bron yn tyfu'n fawr'. The 'yn' in this instance is intrusive. Say, 'Bron â thyfu'n fawr', or 'Bron tyfu'n fawr'. Similarly, it is incorrect to say, 'Maen nhw bron wedi gorffen'. You never have 'bron' followed by 'wedi' and then the verb noun. A minor error which shows that you are nearly there.

A Welsh-speaking Welshman has now climbed Everest, but as hundreds have stood on the summit, do not expect him to be knighted.

Collecting need not mean purgatory for some

One of the most remarkable men of recent years was Robert Owen, but everybody referred to him as Bob Owen Croesor as he spent most of his life in Croesor, Merionethshire. He earned his living as a clerk in a local quarry, but he was also an antiquarian and a collector of books and manuscripts. Somehow, he found room for them all at his home and they were to be found in every room. He specialised in emigrating families and Americans who wished to know their roots often called to see him. Indeed it is said that he seemed to know everything about everybody. He was a popular lecturer and travelled all over Wales, more often than not thumbing lifts as he never owned a car. A society of bibliophiles and collectors established in 1976 is known as 'Cymdeithas Bob Owen'. It publishes its own magazine, *Y Casglwr.*

The Welsh for 'to collect' is 'casglu' and the word is usually used to describe this activity, e.g., 'Roedd Bob Owen yn casglu llyfrau'. But you could hear, 'Dw i'n casglu dy fod ti'n hoffi casglu llyfre' (I gather that you like collecting books). You might also hear people say, 'Rwy'n hel llyfre', as 'hel' can also mean 'to collect', but 'hel' often has a wider meaning and usually refers to a more random form of collecting. A current television programme is called *Hel Straeon*. In it, 'hel' refers to collecting stories but you could say that the programme researchers are 'chasing' these stories as 'hel' can sometimes be a shortened form of 'hela' (to hunt).

'Hel' can also mean 'to spend' and a mother might tell her child who is on the way to the fair, 'Paid hel dy arian ar sbwriel'. 'Hel' appears in a little used saying, 'Hel ei draed'. If a person is loitering somewhere, you could say about him, 'Mae e'n hel ei draed (loitering) yn y pentre'.

Bob Owen often said humorously that some infamous Welsh people could well be in hell, but it is needless to say that there is no relationship between 'hel' and that centrally heated establishment.

Blaming a guard in Cardigan Bay is important

Legend tells us that there was once a thriving city where Cardigan Bay is today. It was guarded by a dike, and twice a day, before the oncoming tide, it was necessary to shut the dike doors. One night this task was entrusted to a habitual drunkard, Seithennin, and after hours of drunken revelry with his friends, he forgot his duties. Consequently the city was flooded and everybody was drowned. On a quiet summer's evening, if you stand on the shores of Cardigan Bay you may well hear the church bells of that unfortunate city pealing from below. We know that this was all Seithennin's fault and that there should be a moral somewhere.

But there is also a lesson for the unwary here. The Welsh for 'bay' is 'bae'. 'Cardigan Bay' is 'Bae Ceredigion' but the Welsh for 'blame', which is 'bai', has a sound which is very similar to the unpracticed ear and it could confuse. You could say, 'Ar Seithennin (yr) oedd y bai' ('It was Seithennin's fault'), but Seithennin could well confess, 'Fy mai i oedd e' ('It was my fault'), with the 'b' taking the soft mutation. He could confuse you more by saying, 'Rwy'n gwybod mai fy mai i oedd e'. Here the first 'mai' means 'that' and the second means 'fault/blame'. The verb noun is 'beio' and you could say, 'Rwy'n beio Seithennin'.

There is a common saying in Welsh which includes 'bai'. We could say, 'Heb os nac oni bai' (Without an 'if' or a 'but for') 'roedd bai arno fe'. Or you might suggest, 'Oni bai am y cwrw, fe fydde Cantre'r Gwaelod (The Sunken Hundred) ar wyneb y dŵr heddiw'. Remember, always write 'oni bai' (two separate words) and not 'oni bae', a common error.

There is a useful Welsh proverb which says, 'Heb ei fai heb ei eni'. (Roughly translated it means: The blameless one is yet to be born.)

And there hangs the moral, I expect, if we wish to blame somebody. Always dilute your beer with plenty of water.

When using your nose, smell well

Many years ago the barker was an important craftsman in Wales. There were two dozen barkers working in Ceredigion alone in 1890. The barker maintained a close contact with the tanneries, of which there were nine in Ceredigion around this time. The barkers stripped the oaks of their barks so that they could obtain the tannin (or barking fluid) from them. Barking was a long, complicated process. Animal hide would be soaked in tannin for up to three years and passers-by would be very aware of this process as they could smell a tannery from a distance. Indeed, because of the smells, tanneries in close proximity to villages were unpopular.

The Welsh for 'to smell' is 'arogli', but the word is often reserved to refer to the most pleasant smells that you could experience. Whilst smelling a rose, you could say, 'Mae'r rhosyn yn arogli'n hyfryd'. The word 'smel' (an obvious borrowing from the English) is also very popular, together with the verb 'smelo'. Again, 'smelo' is often used to describe smelling unpleasant smells and a nineteenth-century traveller might say, 'Mae'r tanerdy'n smelo'n ddrwg'. The verb is often allied to hearing and people often say, 'Rwy'n clywed smel neis'. This is just a common expression, not an example of supernatural abilities.

You might also hear the verb 'gwyntio' or 'gwynto' from the Welsh noun for 'wind' (gwynt). People might say, 'Mae'r draeniau'n gwynto'n gas', but if we wish to say that something exudes a very unpleasant smell, we might say, 'Ma' fe'n drewi'. Or we could use the noun form and ask, 'O ble mae'r drewdod 'ma'n dod?'

Ceredigion bark was much favoured in England and was shipped in sailing ships from ports like Aberystwyth and Cardigan to Bristol, ships that depended on the wind. If you wish to suggest to someone in open air conversation that it is windy, never say, 'Mae'n gwyntio'. He/she might well think that you are suggesting an investment in a bar of soap.

Can Welsh cobs speak Welsh?

For many years lecturers in Welsh departments of our universities lectured on the Welsh language through the medium of English. The first person to dispense with this fashion was Professor W J Gruffydd at Cardiff. He entered his Welsh class one morning and briefly informed his students that he would thereafter be lecturing in Welsh. Gradually the other university colleges followed suit.

I have previously (page 21) referred to the difference between the noun 'Cymraeg' and the adjective 'Cymreig'. The noun refers to the spoken language and it operates in a sentence such as, 'Dw i'n dysgu Cymraeg'.

When some people refer to the Welsh department in a university they say, 'Yr Adran Gymraeg' (the department where things are being done through the medium of Welsh), but others prefer 'Adran y Gymraeg' (the department where the Welsh language is studied). People describe a primary school where Welsh is the main medium of instruction (even though English is taught there) as an 'Ysgol Gymraeg'. At one time a secondary school where Welsh was the medium of instruction (even though English was taught there) was an 'Ysgol Uwchradd Gymraeg', but such a school is now referred to as an 'Ysgol Ddwyieithog'.

Some people refer wishfully to parts of Wales where the Welsh way of life is still dominant as 'Y Fro Gymraeg' but as English is also spoken there it would be more correct to say, 'Y Fro Gymreig'. Like 'Y Swyddfa Gymraeg', 'Y Fro Gymraeg' does not exist. When we describe a Welsh folk song, we say, 'cân werin Gymraeg' but though the words are in the Welsh language, 'Cymraeg', the melody is 'Cymreig'. So adhering to the rules can be confusing.

But if someone in the Royal Welsh Show enthuses to you about 'y cobiau Cymraeg' ask if you can hear the Welsh-speaking cobs in conversation, and never refer to a Welsh cake as 'teisen Gymraeg'.

A matter of two bridges that has arisen

Thomas Telford is well known in Wales because he built Menai Bridge (known locally as 'Pont y Borth'). However, nothing of his bridge remains today. Over the years, the roadway has been widened and sections replaced or renovated, but it still bears his name.

He also built a bridge at Betws-y-coed. As the arch was constructed in the same year as the battle of Waterloo, the fact was duly noted in metal lettering set into it. Telford is famous for building bridges (and canals) in England as well.

The colloquial Welsh for 'building a bridge' is 'codi pont'. Very few would say 'adeiladu pont'. Indeed the word 'codi' is very useful in Welsh and can be heard in many expressions. If somebody is convalescing after an illness and starting to go out, you might hear, 'Mae e'n dechre codi allan'. If you wish to get a ticket for a play, you might tell someone, 'Rhaid ifi godi tocyn/ticed i'r ddrama'. If the weather improves after rain, we often say, 'Ma hi'n dechre codi', 'hi' in this instance being the weather, which is always feminine.

Sometimes, the second person singular in the imperative case is used incorrectly. The word to use is 'cod', but many say 'cwyd'. If a mother calls upon her child to get up from bed at once to go to school, she should say, 'Cod ar unwaith', and not 'Cwyd ar unwaith'. If someone is downhearted, don't say to him, 'Cwyd dy galon', but 'Cod dy galon'.

You will find a literary form, 'cyfod', as well. 'Cyfod' and 'cod' have similar meanings but the former is not used in conversation.

Someone should have told Telford that the battle of Waterloo was not fought in Waterloo but in a place four miles from the Belgian town. But he need not be despondent as the subsequent treaty was signed there.

Pont y Borth (Pont Telford)

The story of the bear and the poet

Vicious bears were common in Wales at one time and were hunted for their flesh. Today stuffed, cuddly ones are hunted instead. To cater for this hobby, companies have set up bear factories and one of them moved a few years ago from London to new premises in Pontypool. One of the most popular of its products is a fully jointed bear sporting a red ribbon and a wide smile which possibly widens when it hears tinkling till bells.

The Welsh word for bear is 'arth'. It takes the feminine gender, though the famous tale by Southey is sometimes incorrectly titled *Y Tri Arth*. *Y Tair Arth* is the correct title. There is another feminine form, 'arthes', which is hardly ever used. We tend to say 'arth fenyw' (feminine bear) instead.

There are numerous plural forms of Welsh nouns. Probably the most difficult form for the English speaker (familiar with the simple 'add an s or es') to master is the plural being formed by a prefixed or an internal vowel change, for example, 'arth' usually becomes 'eirth', but you can come across 'arthod' and 'eirthod' as well, as Welsh speakers can also become confused.

A verb noun, 'arthio' is formed from 'arth' and it can mean, 'to scold'. You can reprimand someone by saying, 'Paid ag arthio, da thi'.

Teddy-bear sellers are often poetic in their description of bears. The Welsh for poet is 'bardd' and the plural is formed in the same way as 'arth > eirth', and we have 'bardd > beirdd', the only plural form. A 'bardd' composes a 'cerdd' (poem), but there is no such word as 'ceirdd'. The plural form here is 'cerddi'—just adding an 'i'.

Our Pontypool bear had not accepted its Welsh roots in 1994. The manufacturers stated at that time that it was 'Made in Great Britain', and not 'Gwnaed yng Nghymru'.

A milky welcome on the hillside, perhaps

Many young people today spend hours polishing the chrome badges and metallic paint on their sports cars. Many years ago, their counterparts could well have been devoting such care to their horses. Farmers wished their horses to be seen at their best and they were often taken (suitably adorned) to agricultural shows. Colourful ribbons would be pleated into their manes and there would be shining brasses on their foreheads and collars. They would spend hours on this task, but if you wish to see such brasses today, you will have to look on chimney breasts in farmhouses, or even council houses, relics of bygone days.

I mentioned the word 'bron' (nearly) on page 159. It can also mean 'breast', but never refer to a chimney breast as 'bron y simdde'. 'Bron' (breast) often describes the milk secreting organ of a woman, the plural form being 'bronnau'. The English word 'breast' has also been borrowed as 'brest' and a woman's breasts would be referred to as 'brestiau'. If a child is being breast-fed, a mother might say simply, 'Mae e ar y fron'. The singular form, 'bron' can refer to any bosom, even a male one, but you would not use a plural form here and say, 'Ma fe ar y bronnau'. A name for 'robin red breast' is 'brongoch'.

In response to a question, 'Ble mae'r ceffyl?' you might hear, 'Mae e ar y fron'. This would mean that it is on the hillside and not that it is being breast-fed. The word appears in place-names and Bronnant and Fron-deg (a mutated form) are examples that come to mind. But this 'bron' has a different plural form, 'bronnydd', which is hardly ever used orally.

The Welsh noun 'bronglwm' for a ribboned knot on the breast has been adopted by many as a Welsh word for *brassiere* though some people have wittily suggested that the place-name Froncysyllte would serve just as well.

What a to do about a rugby stadium

There was once a hostelry in Cardiff called The Cardiff Arms Hotel. It reminds us of the times when knights wore coats of arms (arfbeisiau) in battles so that they could be recognised. In 1878, it was demolished to make way for the widening of Castle Street, but, in memory of that hostelry, the Cardiff Rugby Club baptised its new ground Cardiff Arms Park. The Welsh name given to the ground at a later date was 'Parc yr Arfau', but the translator made a mistake as the word 'arms' does not refer to weapons. To be technically correct, we should come to Parc yr Arfbeisiau to see a game of rugby, but oral tradition has given 'Parc yr Arfau' (Parc yr Arfe) universal popularity.

Originally, the Welsh verb noun for 'to make' was 'gwneuthur' and the Welsh verb noun for 'to come' was 'dyfod'. These two forms still appear in literary forms, but over the years they have been superseded by simpler oral forms, 'gwneuthur' becoming 'gwneud' and 'dyfod' becoming 'dod'. Nobody today would say, 'Wyt ti'n dyfod i'r gêm fory?' Similarly, the literary form 'dywedyd' (to say) has given ground to the oral form 'dweud', but you will find still other oral variations that could well confuse you. People in north Wales tend to say 'deud' (dropping the 'w'), and you could well hear the expression, 'Tewch â deud!' (You don't say!). If they wish to agree with a statement which you have made, they might say, 'Deudwch chi', or even 'Dudwch chi', in the second person singular, present tense. Similarly, 'gwneud' often loses its internal 'w' and you might be asked, 'Be ti'n neud?'—the 'g' being subject to mutation. Even 'dod' has not escaped changes, and you could well hear, 'Wyt ti'n dŵad i'r dafarn?'

Nobody comes to the Cardiff Arms Park to see an international match today. It is still there, just around the corner, but the main pitch is now referred to (correctly) as Y Maes Cenedlaethol.

Now is not the time for spooning

The Mabinogion tells us that Pwyll Pendefig Dyfed loved to hunt in Cwm Cuch in north Pembrokeshire. Many years later the village of Aber-cuch became famous for its wood turners, mainly as there was a plentiful supply of sycamore (masarn) in the area. Sycamore was the most popular wood in the manufacture of utensils in the home as it did not leave any taste on dairy products. Before the beginning of the First World War, the village was a hive of industry, but now there is nothing there to show how busy it once was. Now, plastic reigns supreme.

People often have to use the Welsh word(s) for 'now' in conversation. In South Wales, we use 'nawr' and in north Wales we use 'rŵan'. As it happens, 'rŵan' is 'nawr' spelt backwards, the 'w' in 'rŵan' carrying the circumflex, but there is no truth in the tradition that north Walians deliberately reversed the word in order to confuse people, as 'nawr' and 'rŵan' come from separate roots. 'Nawr' is a shortened form of 'yn awr', the 'y' having been dropped. We often say and write 'yn awr' today. We could write, 'Does dim llwyau pren yn y siop yn awr', or 'Does dim amser gen i nawr'. 'Rŵan', on the other hand, comes from 'yr awr hon' (this hour).

You will find that many people will begin a sentence with the expression, 'Nawr 'te' (south Wales) or 'Rŵan, 'ta' (north Wales), the ''te/'ta' being the shortened form of 'ynte(u)' which can mean 'then'—the Welsh equivalent of 'now then'. When you are advised to do something, people might tell you, 'Nawr yw'r amser/Rŵan yw'r amser'.

Young men all over Wales would carve an intricate love spoon from the wood of the sycamore to declare their love for their favourite maiden. Now, 'spooning' in the traditional sense has gone and stone has superseded wood as a girl's best friend. More expensive, too.

An accommodation problem for a giant

Giants abound in Welsh folk tales. One of the most famous is Bendigeidfran the half brother of Branwen (White crow). He arranged an unfortunate marriage for her with Matholwch, a king in Ireland. Matholwch abused her as he thought he had been insulted by Branwen's brother, Efnisien, during the wedding feast. After Branwen had sent a starling (drudwen) to inform Bendigeidfran about her predicament, he led an army to avenge the wrong done to his half sister and many died in the resulting battle; a very sad tale.

We are told that Bendigeidfran was a giant who could not live in a house. It was necessary to erect a huge tent (pabell) for him.

'Yn' (in) and 'mewn' (in) can be very confusing for the learner as they are not interchangeable. A useful rule might be that the name that follows 'yn' (often + y) is specific. You would say, 'Mae'r plant yn y babell nawr'. But remember that this 'yn' becomes 'ym' in certain instances, for example, you would say, 'Mae'r gêm ym Mangor dydd Sadwrn' (without + y).

You will also use 'yn' before a noun that is followed by another noun, for example, 'Roedd tân yn ysgol y pentre neithiwr'.

It now follows that you should use 'mewn' in a non-specific situation, for example, 'Doedd Bendigeidfran ddim yn byw mewn tŷ. Roedd e'n byw mewn pabell', or, 'Rhaid iti roi'r dillad mewn dŵr poeth i'w golchi nhw'.

But in certain situations, a noun that follows a noun operates as an adjective and not as a noun. In such instances, 'mewn' is acceptable, and you could say, 'Mae e'n mynd i'r gwaith mewn bỳs gweithwyr' (. . . a bus for workers).

'Rhai' and 'llawer' are unspecific words and you should use 'mewn' in front of them, for example, 'Mae'r cawr mewn llawer stori', or, 'Mae cewri'n byw mewn rhai pebyll'.

You will be aware that it was Bendigeidfran who uttered the famous phrase, 'A fo ben bid bont', as he lay across a magic river. Had he fallen in, he would have been 'yn y dŵr', as well as 'mewn dŵr'.

Drops and drops of rain generate dams

Wales could well be described as a land of reservoirs. At one time, Claerwen dam, in the old Radnorshire, which supplies water for Birmingham, was the highest in Europe. During the Second World War, this particular dam was used as target practice by the bombers who later went on to attack various dams in the Ruhr valley in Germany, dropping the famous bouncing bombs invented by Barnes Wallis. Not all the enemy dams were breached during these raids. Many years ago, a dam at Dolgarrog in north Wales was breached by the elements. Water poured from it down the valley, causing much damage and some loss of life. You will hardly ever see water pouring over Clywedog dam above Llanidloes as it is a control dam.

Water pouring from Dolgarrog dam would have been a dramatic sight. Sightseers might well have said, 'Roedd e'n tywallt i lawr y dyffryn', 'tywallt' being the north Wales word for 'to pour'. A tea-time question in Bangor might be, 'Ga(f) i dywallt te i chi?' or yet again, 'Ga(f) i dollti llefrith ichi?' 'Tollti' is a colloquial variation of 'tywallt'. In rainy weather, they might say, 'Mae hi'n tywallt y glaw'. But if the weather is very bad indeed, they might say, 'Ma hi'n tresio bwrw'.

South Walians use a different word, 'arllwys'. If it is raining very heavily, they will say, 'Mae'n 'i harllwys hi', there being no reference to the word 'glaw' (rain). They could well use another word, 'diwel'. This can mean 'pour' or 'empty' but the second definition is rarely used. People often say, 'Mae hi'n diwel y glaw!'

You will know that in English it rains cats and dogs but that in Wales, we say, 'Ma hi'n bwrw hen wragedd a ffyn'. We also say, 'bwrw cyllyll a ffyrc'.

But whichever way we describe this falling water, much of it is ultimately piped to teapots and bath tubs in England.

Old can be old and also not so old

If you travel between Cwmystwyth and Devil's Bridge in Ceredigion you will proceed under an old looking arch. It was sometimes referred to locally as the 'Roman Arch', though the local inhabitants were aware that it had been built in the eighteenth century to open the way to vast acres of reclaimed land. The owner, Thomas Johnes, was a pioneering gentleman farmer who had built his mansion (Yr Hafod = summer abode) on the banks of the river Ystwyth. He was a staunch supporter of the agrarian revolution and as this arch was built around the time of the enthronement of George III (Farmer George), a few people speculated that it was a commemorative one.

You will be familiar with the Welsh adjective 'hen' for 'old'. It appears in 'hendre' (old abode), the opposite of 'hafod', a fact which I mentioned on page 43.

But treat it warily as it has fluctuating meanings. I mention on page 22 that 'hen ddyn' means 'old man', the adjective (this being exceptional) coming before the noun. In such an instance if it comes after the noun (dyn hen) it suggests that a man is very old and you can say 'hen ddyn hen' (or 'hen ŵr hen'). But if you describe someone as 'hen lanc' you are merely saying that he has not (yet) entered the marriage stakes.

If we wish to say that a person is growing old, we would say, 'Mae e'n mynd yn hen', or 'Ma fe'n heneiddio'. If a child is very forward for his/her age, we say, 'Mae e/hi'n henaidd', but what you would hear would be 'henedd' as the 'ai' often erodes to 'e' in conversation.

But 'hen' can often be used as a sentence filler, and you could hear, 'Mae'r hen blant wedi mynd i'r ysgol yn barod'. Here, 'hen' has no specific meaning.

Again, if things do not turn out as you might expect them to do, people might commiserate by saying 'Hen dro', 'tro' here meaning a turn/twist in events. 'Hen' here does not mean 'old'.

If a cup of tea has been cold for a long time, you can say, 'Ma fe wedi hen oeri', or if you are tired of reading this, you can say, 'Rwy'i 'di hen flino . . .'

Yr Arch, Cwmystwyth, Ceredigion

173

Little drips to make you know

One of the earliest Welsh poets was known as Taliesin (White forehead). Many tales have been woven around him and it is difficult to separate fact from fiction. One such tale says that at one time he was called Gwion Bach. He had the task of assisting blind Mordaf to guard a cauldron of magic broth concocted by the witch Ceridwen. This was to boil for a year and a day. After that time, a drop would be sufficient to give anyone knowledge of all things. She had prepared this for her ugly son, Afagddu (Jet black), but after a contrived accident one hot drop fell on Gwion's hand. He sucked at it—and became a great poet.

The Welsh for 'drop' is 'diferyn'. Both the singular and the plural form (diferion) are used often in Welsh. If you are not very partial to milk and are invited by someone to tea, you might be asked if you take milk. As you only want the tiniest drop, you will respond, 'Dim ond diferyn bach', the adjective 'bach' giving added emphasis. You would not say, 'Dim ond diferion bach'. If you wish to draw attention to a leaking trough under the eaves, you could say, 'Mae diferion o law'n disgyn o'r cafn', but is some parts of Wales you might come across a colloquial word for 'cafn' which does not appear in all dictionaries. This word is 'lander', and you could say, 'Mae dŵr yn diferu o'r lander/landeri'. 'Lander' often becomes 'landar' in conversation. Note also that the verb noun 'diferu' (to drip) is often used in Welsh and that 'cafn' is used also to describe a food trough or a similar utensil. If you wish to say that you are soaked to the skin, you would say, 'Dw i'n wlyb diferu', the Welsh for 'dripping wet'.

At a typical Welsh farmhouse meal there is nothing like cawl dripping from a ladle, or 'cawl yn diferu o'r lletwad'.

Remember if you wish to stop, kneel and sit

William Salesbury, one of the greatest Welshmen who ever lived, was responsible for preparing a few of the first books ever published in Welsh; one was *The Book of Common Prayer* (*Y Llyfr Gweddi Gyffredin*). Unfortunately, William Salesbury had a somewhat idiosyncratic style, and Bishop William Morgan had to revise this work before it became a popular service book in Welsh churches. In a revised form, this book is still used in Welsh churches (not chapels). If you peruse a bilingual copy you will see three imperative forms in certain sections of the English version where worshippers are expected to stand, kneel or sit.

The Welsh section offers: 'sefyll' (to stand), 'penlinio' (to kneel), 'eistedd' (to sit). These are not imperative forms but they may serve as a warning to language learners as the verb noun is sometimes the same as the imperative form, although this is not always the case. For example, the verb noun 'aros' (to stand) is also the imperative form first person singular, and if someone is going too quickly, you could say, 'aros funud'. But if you wish someone to stand still, you would not say, 'Sefyll yn llonydd', but 'Saf yn llonydd', 'sefyll' not being an imperative form. In conversation, many might say, 'Sa'n llonydd'. If you wish someone to kneel, you would say, 'Penlinia', and if you wish a person to sit, you would say, 'Eistedd', though many people might say, 'Eistedda'.

But the 'sefyll' of the *Llyfr Gweddi Gyffredin* (not 'Llyfr Gweddi Cyffredin') is quite correct and acceptable. Generally, it means, 'you are to stand'. 'Penlinio' means 'you are to kneel' and 'Eistedd' means 'you are to sit'. If children are prone to run in a school corridor, a teacher can command, 'cerddwch', or use the verb noun, 'cerdded', the latter being a reminder rather than a command.

The verb noun for 'to remember' is 'cofio'. Cofiwch!

You sometimes have to make bones about it

Up to the beginning of this century, people with bone fractures fared badly as orthopaedic techniques had not been developed. One of the most important pioneering doctors in this field was Robert Jones who was born in Rhyl in 1857. He studied medicine in Liverpool, and did more than anybody during the Great War to treat soldiers with bone fractures correctly, developing what became known as the 'Thomas Splints'. His successful techniques were copied by hospitals all over Britain and in 1917 he was knighted for his work. The Robert Jones Memorial Hospital near Oswestry bears testimony to his name.

Bones can cause problems to learners as well. Take the ankle, for example. The dictionary, *Gair i Gall,* offers 'ffêr', as a familiar Welsh word, but another widely used word is 'pigwrn'. In *Y Geiriadur Cymraeg Cyfoes* this is described as 'cone, pinnacle', with no reference to 'ankle'. 'Pigwrn' is found often in a mutated form and you would say, 'Mae e wedi torri'i bigwrn'. But in some areas, the ankle is referred to as 'bigwrn' and you could also hear, 'Mae e wedi ysigo (to sprain) ei figwrn'. This is not an example, therefore, of an initial letter being mutated (wrongly) twice.

But certain people refer to 'ankle' as 'migwrn', so you can have 'pigwrn' becoming 'bigwrn', and 'bigwrn/migwrn' becoming 'figwrn' in mutated forms. 'Bigwrn' can refer also to a knuckle joint. The wrist is referred to as 'arddwrn', but a 'g' has attached itself to the beginning of the word and you can also hear, 'Mae'i garddwrn hi wedi torri'.

We can use bone joints to explain the closeness of a relationship. In English you may say, 'Blood is thicker than water', but in addition to a literal translation of this in Welsh we have, 'Nes penelin nag arddwrn' (An elbow is nearer than a wrist). A variation is, 'Nes elin (forearm) nag arddwrn'. If all this confuses you remember that, grammatically speaking, it is more convenient to break a leg than an ankle!

A *library of plurals to ponder over*

The building with the greatest number of bookshelves in Wales is the National Library of Wales at Aberystwyth. More are having to be added continually to accommodate the books that are delivered daily. The biggest collections there are the Llansteffan Manuscripts, the result of the lifetime's hobby of Sir John Williams, Llansteffan, who was a physician to Queen Victoria. He was knighted for his services in 1894. He gave all his books and manuscripts to the proposed new National Library of Wales which received its royal charter in 1907 and was opened in that year. It moved to the present purpose-built buildings in 1916.

The Welsh for 'bookshelves' (a shelf of books), is 'silff lyfrau' which has the same meaning as the English, 'silff o lyfrau'. If you fancy a fruit salad, you would ask for 'salad ffrwythau', following the same pattern. Books are kept in a 'cwpwrdd llyfrau' and you clean your teeth with a 'brws dannedd'.

Most people, if they like an apple tart (a tart of apples—i.e. a tart of more than one apple) will ask, 'Ga(f) i darten afalau (fale), os gwelwch chi'n dda?' But many will ask (incorrectly) for 'tarten afal'. Similarly, if you wish to spend some money you might ask your bank manager, 'Gaf fi lyfr sieciau, os gwelwch chi'n dda?' It is not as correct to say, 'llyfr siec' as it contains more than one cheque.

A person with a disability who uses a wheel chair (a chair with wheels) might say, 'Mae cadair olwynion gen i', but some might ask, 'Oes cadair olwyn 'da chi?' ignoring the usual pattern. These are examples of incorrect adaptation from the English and should not be encouraged.

Many ask why the National Library is situated in Aberystwyth. It would be difficult to think of a better setting overlooking Cardigan Bay, and the benefactor must have realised this because he stipulated that the gift was conditional upon its being built there—with shelves for more than one book; today there are about 80 miles of them.

About poisons, donkeys and a prime minister

D Lloyd George, the Welsh-speaking prime minister, was famous for turning the tables on hecklers. One day a heckler wished to remind him about his roots, and when the orator was in full flow, he asked, 'Prime Minister, what happened to the donkey and cart that you had when you were young?' Quick as a flash Lloyd George replied, 'I know nothing about the cart but I think I have just found the donkey'.

'About' takes us again to the tricky area of prepositions. The Welsh for 'about' is 'am' but this is one of the prepositions that conjugate, and you could ask when approaching a group, 'Pwy sy'n siarad amdana(f) i?' A reply could be, 'Does neb yn siarad amdanat ti/ amdanoch chi'. If you wish to inform someone that someone is looking for him/her, you would say, 'Mae Alun yn edrych amdanat ti'. It is incorrect to say, 'Mae Alun yn edrych arnat ti', in this instance as 'arnat ti' could mean either 'upon' or 'on'.

In most parts of Wales, if you were looking for the children, you would say, 'Rwy'n edrych am y plant', with no conjugation, but in some parts of Wales, you will find that speakers conjugate (incorrectly) and they will say, 'Rwy'n edrych amdan y plant', with the accent on the ultimate syllable.

If you are going out for the evening with someone and you wish him/her to wait for you, the expression to use is, 'Arhoswch amdana(f) i'. But you might well hear the incorrect expression, 'Arhoswch i fi'.

Tradition states also that a lady shouted at Lloyd George during one of his orations, 'If I were your wife, I'd give you poison.' He replied, 'Madam, if I were your husband, I'd take it', but it is impossible to say how true such stories are. The 'poison' yarn has been told about others, including Winston Churchill.

Never think of sex going down hill

The biggest castle in Wales is Caerffili Castle. In the 1930s it was described by Miss Edith Picton Tuberviller, a descendant of one of the Norman invaders of Glamorgan as 'the largest ruin in Western Europe'. The most famous feature of the partially restored edifice is the leaning tower. It is fifty feet high and is at least nine feet out of the perpendicular, rivalling even the leaning tower of Pisa. Nobody knows how it came to slope or lean over. It was most probably subjected to a gunpowder attack during the Civil War and is a tribute to the masons who built it.

There are many Welsh words for 'slope'. A famous tourist quarry in Blaenau Ffestiniog is named Llechwedd Quarry', or 'The Quarry of the Incline'. You could say, using the plural form, 'Mae defaid yn pori'r llechweddau'.

Another much used word is 'llethr' and a Welsh expression which suggests a steep hill would be, 'llethr serth', the plural here being 'llethrau'. Another word for 'slope', much used in north Wales' is 'gallt', but you might well see a mutated form (losing the 'g') which is 'yr allt'. In north Wales, if a person is losing his health, people might say, 'Mae o'n mynd i lawr yr allt'. The same word is used in south Wales. There, it usually means a wooded slope. In south Wales, a slope that is not wooded would be described as 'rhiw', and you could say, 'Mae'r rhiw rhyw filltir o hyd'. Note the spelling here, and the difference between 'rhiw' (hill, slope) and 'rhyw' (some).

Describing Caerffili tower, we might say, 'Mae e ar oledd(f)', or, 'Ma fe'n goleddfu dros naw troedfedd'. In conversation, people often say 'goleddu', ignoring the 'f'. You might well come across this word in your Welsh lessons as 'goleddfu' is the Welsh expression for 'modify'.

I should add that 'rhyw' can also mean 'sex', a kind of slippery slope for a few.

Pirates could well have come to steal Bardsey Isle

I have mentioned Bardsey Isle (Ynys Enlli) off the Llŷn (not Lleyn) peninsula in Gwynedd before. We consider it a holy island because of the saints that are buried there, but nothing is ever what it seems and for years it was a popular base for smugglers. They used to land there and people would come to them to buy their spoils. The wily plunderers rarely came to the mainland.

You will know that the Welsh for 'to come' is 'dod'. The word can be as wily as the buccaneers themselves in its various forms; and despite these varieties, we introduce still more in conversation. If we wish to say, 'He will not come tonight', using a correct grammatical form we would state, ''Ddaw e ddim heno' (note that the apostrophe before 'Ddaw' warns you that the 'Ni' has been omitted in a negative structure), but what you might well hear is a corrupt form, ''Ddeiff e ddim heno'.

There are two verb noun forms, 'dod' and 'dyfod'. I state on page 168 that you will hardly ever hear the more literary 'dyfod' in conversation but you could well meet the structure in a reference to newcomers to a locality. Someone might say, 'Newydd-ddyfodiaid ydyn nhw'. Others might say, 'Pobol ddŵad ydyn nhw' (They are people who have come). In certain parts of Wales, people who have been in residence for many years are still referred to as 'pobol ddŵad'.

You could well be confronted by a choice in the imperative case as well. In some parts of Wales, you will hear, 'Dewch yma', in others you will hear, 'Dowch yma'. There is a third choice in the realms of poetry. A well known Welsh carol begins, 'O deuwch, ffyddloniaid' (O come all ye faithful).

If you don't know where you are with all these versions, take heart as Ynys Enlli could sympathise with you. In the seventeenth century, many insisted that it really belonged to Pembrokeshire, but Pembrokeshire later said that Caernarfonshire was welcome to it.

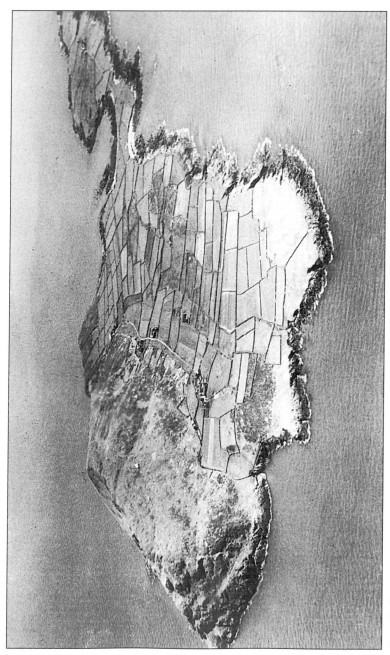

Ynys Enlli

Beware when people bring gifts

The annual Lampeter and Pontrhydfendigaid eisteddfodau are referred to as Eisteddfodau Teulu Pantyfedwen. There are also Pantyfedwen Trusts to assist people who require financial assistance in certain instances. All these originated with Sir David James who was brought up at Pantyfedwen, a farmhouse not far from Strata Florida Abbey, Pontrhydfendigaid, before going to London to make a fortune from dealing in the grain trade and running cinemas in the West End. He gave the Welsh League of Youth a magnificent silver trophy for a soccer competition for youngsters, and the Grand Hotel (now demolished) in Borth, Ceredigion.

The Welsh for 'to give' is 'rhoddi' or 'rhoi'—both words having the same meaning. You can use the root form 'rhodd' upon which to build other useful words. You could start with the root word by itself, and say, 'Rydw i wedi prynu rhodd (gift) i Mam'. When reference is made to a gift in a publication, you might read, 'Roedd y Grand Hotel yn rhoddedig gan Syr David James'. The name for the giver is 'rhoddwr/ rhoddwraig' and you could say, 'Fe/Hi yw rhoddwr/rhoddwraig y cwpan'. The plural is 'rhoddion', and we could say, 'Mae Syr David James, y rhoddwr mawr, wedi rhoi llawer o roddion i eisteddfodau Cymru'. The 'rh' mutates in certain instances, and you would say, 'Mae rhaid i fi roi anrheg iddo fe' or 'Roddest ti anrheg iddi hi?'

You will hardly ever hear 'rhoddi' in conversation, 'rhoi' being the most commonly used word. But a few speakers (and writers) have an incorrect tendency to add a 'd' to this word, and you could hear, 'Mae'n rhoid llawer o arian i'r capel bob blwyddyn'.

Though a generous benefactor, Sir James more often than not attached a condition (amod) to his gifts. He was knighted for his generosity and was happy to be called 'Sir James', but you could sometimes hear 'Sir Amod' as an aside as well. He lies under a magnificent monument in Strata Florida churchyard.

A much maligned author is now revered

Caradoc Evans was born in 1878 in Llanfihangel-ar-Arth, Carmarthen-shire. His father had died when he was young and he himself had an unhappy and impoverished childhood. He blamed what he described as narrow religious bigotry for much of this and left home to seek his fortune as soon as he could. After working for some time in Cardiff, he left for London and became a journalist. In 1915, he published a collection of virulent short stories, *My People*, sharply criticising the Welsh way of life. In 1923 he wrote a play, *Taffy* but this was booed off the London stage after one performance.

The Welsh for the verb noun 'to have' is 'cael'. It is a much used and sometimes eroded irregular verb. Using the third person singular, past tense, you could say simply, 'Cefais i gig i ginio heddiw', but others might say, 'Fe/Mi gefais i . . .' Others might erode the verb and say, 'Fe ge(fai)s i amser da yn y dre'.

'Cânt fynd i'r ysgol yn y car', is a common literary form, but in conversation, people would say, 'Fe gân nhw fynd i'r gwely'n gynnar heno'.

The impersonal form of the present tense is 'ceir'. Using this form you might say, 'Fe geir cwrw da yn y dafarn yna', but there is no relationship at all between the verb 'ceir' and the plural noun 'ceir' for 'car'. You could say, 'Ceir ceir i fynd â'r plant i'r ysgol'. The impersonal form of the past tense is 'cafwyd' or 'caed'. 'Cafwyd' is the most popular verb form and a report might state, 'Fe gafwyd digon o fwyd yn y briodas'. If someone wishes to say that he escaped by the skin of his teeth he would say, 'Cael a chael oedd hi'. You will come across the mutated verb noun, preceded by 'ar' in notices. Look out for, 'Tocynnau'r Loteri Genedlaethol ar gael yma'.

Caradog Evans escaped by the skin of his teeth from the London theatre after the performance of *Taffy* but people today feel that he has been misunderstood and that he should be accepted as a prominent literary figure.

The little saucepan boils, but where?

It is said that the 'second' national anthem of Wales was first sung in a *noson lawen* in Llanwrtyd in 1895, but nobody seems to know who composed it. Even though Llanelli is referred to as 'tref y sosban' it is possible that there was no relationship initially between the town and song, but in those days, miners from Llanelli would have been in this spa on holiday many times. It is possible that they sang the song on their way back to Llanelli and that it rooted there. Llanwrtyd cannot claim it as it is said that a student from Bangor had been in the village at the same time and had brought the first verse to a merry evening, the only one composed at the time, and it is said that this student's roots were in Llanelli. More than one author claim the authorship of various other parts of the song.

'Have been in' translates as 'wedi bod yn' and here we are in the realms of the present perfect continuous form of the verb 'to be' + 'yn', which can cause pitfalls to those who translate directly from English. A common English expression would be, 'I have been to the class many times'. This can translate wrongly, almost word for word as, 'Rydw i wedi bod i'r dosbarth sawl gwaith'. Here the snag is 'to the'. In Welsh this does not translate as 'i'r' (to the). The Welsh structure should be, 'Rydw i wedi bod yn y dosbarth sawl gwaith'. Similarly, you should say, 'Rydw i wedi bod yn Llanwrtyd', and not 'Rydw i wedi bod i Lanwrtyd', or 'Dw i 'di bod yn y gwaith' (and not '. . . i'r gwaith'). This usually occurs when you refer to a specific place.

There is a shortened form which can also cause pitfalls. You can say, 'Bues i yn Llanelli'n gweld y gêm', but not, 'Bues i i Lanelli'n . . .' 'Bues' is a colloquial form, the literary form being 'bûm'. The circumflex here is important as the word can be confused with the mutated form of 'five' (bum(p)).

A real saucepanful of pitfalls. No wonder the cat lost its temper!

Eleanor can help you have a roof over your head

Eleanor, the wife of Llywelyn ap Gruffydd (often referred to as Llywelyn the Last (Prince of Wales), had a short but tempestuous life. Her father, Simon de Montford, an enemy of King Edward, arranged for her to marry the Welsh prince who was much older than she was. In 1275 she sailed from France to her betrothal in north Wales but her boat was captured by the king's men. She was eventually freed in 1278 as Llywelyn had by then promised to pay fealty to Edward. She died giving birth to her only child, Gwenllian, in June 1282.

'Eleanor' can be used to help people combat many of the circumflexing problems in Welsh. In words of one syllable the a, e, o, u, w, y vowel sounds before the consonants l, n, r are sometimes short, sometimes long. These consonants appear in this order in the proper noun, Eleanor, and helps us to bear them in mind. When the vowels are long, we circumflex them, for example we can say, 'Mae merch lân ar lan y llyn yn Llŷn', or, 'Dyw'r llyn yn Llŷn ddim mor ddwfn â'r môr'. There are hardly any similarly spelt words with both long and short vowels ending in 'r' but the same rule applies and we could say, 'Mae'r gêr pysgota ger y drws'. As 'i' is nearly always long, it is hardly ever circumflexed.

People often circumflex vowels unnecessarily, for example Llandaf is often written as Llandâf. There is no need to circumflex the vowels in 'ras', 'haf', 'nos', etc. The vowel in 'to' (roof) is not circumflexed, nor is the 'w' in 'sw', but the 'y' in 'tŷ' is an exception as the mutated form 'dŷ' could be confused with 'dy' ('your').

There are two exceptions, 'dyn' (man) and 'hen' (old), and you could say, 'Mae'r hen ddyn yn bwyta hufen iâ yn y sw'.

It was hoped that Gwenllian would help solve the problems of the Welsh following the death of her father, but she was whisked away to England and died in Sempringham Abbey in Lincolnshire, without having had the satisfaction of having had a Welsh roof over her head.

Let us idle over a cuppa

William Williams, Pantycelyn, Carmarthenshire was the most prolific of our hymn writers. He was one of the leaders of the Welsh Methodist revival in the early eighteenth century, and this involved establishing societies all over Wales at a time when travelling was difficult due to the nature of the roads. Usually, he went on horseback. He was an astute businessman and always carried a selection of his hymn-booklets with him, to be sold to the converted. He also carried a supply of tea, a drink which was becoming cheaper and popular at that time. This also sold well.

We still like our 'paned o de', but the tea should be infused properly and allowed to stand before the liquid is poured. Under the influence of English, many will say, 'Rhaid gadael i'r te sefyll', but there is an entirely Welsh expression, 'Rhaid gadael i'r te fwrw'i ffrwyth'. Literally, this means 'casting its fruit', and does not translate. Listen for, 'Rwy'n hoffi i'r te fwrw'i ffrwyth'. In some parts of north Wales, you might hear another expression in a question such as, 'Ydi'r te 'di trwytho?' You will find that 'trwyth' can be translated as 'infusion'.

I have mentioned previously that the word 'bwrw' crops up in many Welsh idioms, such as 'bwrw'r Sul' for 'weekend'. In north Wales, people who have vomited would say, ''Dw i 'di bwrw i fyny' (or 'taflu i fyny'). If a visitor at your home expresses a wish to depart, she might say, 'Rhaid i fi'i bwrw hi'. This expression is most common in south Wales. It is also used as 'assuming'. Listen for, 'A bwrw na fydd hi'n bwrw glaw, fyddi di'n dod?' Again, if a cat or dog is losing its hairs, explain, 'Mae e/hi'n bwrw'i f/blew'. If you are gradually coming out of a period of grief, people might say for you, 'Mae e/hi'n bwrw'i hiraeth'.

Indeed there are as many choices as there are of tea leaves!

Take counting into account and think of goats

I referred to the famous nonsense song, a favourite with Welsh Male Voice Choirs, 'Oes gafr eto?' on page 35. A rendering of this song could well be useful in parts of north Wales where feral goats still roam.

Mae'n anodd cyfrif y geifr sydd yn Eryri a'r Gogarth yn Llandudno a Chadair Idris a mannau eraill. Maen nhw'n cuddio yn y creigiau. Mae pobl yn amcangyfrif (to estimate) fod tuag un fil a phum cant o eifr gwyllt yng Ngwynedd. A few conservationists have suggested that they should be controlled, but others do not wish to see them culled.

The word 'cyfrif' can be as wily as the goats. Mae gan nifer o bobol gyfrif banc (bank account), ac rydyn ni'n aml yn amcangyfrif faint sydd yn ein cyfrif banc. Mae plant yn cyfrif (to count) yn yr ysgol. Os ydy person yn ddrwg, mae'n cael ei alw i gyfrif (call to account) ambell dro. Gallwch glywed, 'Mae rhai wedi galw aelodau o Fwrdd yr Iaith i gyfrif am siarad Saesneg mewn cyfarfodydd'.

Pan fyddwch yn dadlau, fe all person ofyn, 'Ydy fy marn i'n cyfrif?' (Is my opinion of any consequence?) Os yw rhywun yn gofyn i chi, 'Gaf fi ddod i'r cwrdd heno?' fe allwch chi ateb, 'Ar bob cyfrif!' Mae pobl yn dweud heddiw, 'Ar bob cyfrif, rhaid gwario mwy o arian ar ysgolion'. Ambell dro, mae pobl yn dweud 'ar gyfrif' yn lle 'o achos' neu 'oherwydd'. Gallwch ddweud, 'Mae Dafydd yn cyfrif y geifr ar gyfrif ei allu i gyfrif anifeiliaid'.

Os oes cyfrif gyda chi mewn siop, neu gerdyn credyd, mae'n rhaid ichi dalu dyledion (debts) nawr ac yn y man, hynny yw, mae'n rhaid i chi wastatáu'r cyfrif—talu'r bil.

Cofiwch, peidiwch â gadael i afr ddod i'r ardd ar unrhyw gyfrif! Mae gafr yn bwyta popeth! Mae'r bobl sy'n byw yn Eryri'n gwybod hynny!

187

So let us drink as we go

The magnificent tomb of Sir Benjamin Hall, a staunch friend of the Welsh language, may be seen in Llanofer village churchyard, Monmouthshire. Tradition maintains that the clock bell, Big Ben, was named after him. A padlocked grating is set in the ground nearby; this guards steps that lead down to the vault. At his burial, people thought that Sir Ben might be thirsty on his journey to heaven, so they placed a bottle of wine by the coffin. A few years ago thieves invaded the tomb. Later, people discovered an empty wine bottle by the coffin and assumed that the thieves had drunk its contents. Therefore, a stronger padlock was affixed to the grating.

The Welsh for 'therefore/so' is 'felly' but many Welsh speakers choose to ignore this word and plump for the English 'so' instead. This is not a recent development but its use can be confusing to the learner, especially if it is linked with another colloquial expression, for example, 'es'. This is the third person singular past tense of 'mynd' a very irregular verb form. The literary form is 'euthum'. This is the most commonly written form and you must familiarise yourself with it, but nearly everybody tends to say 'es' in conversation. Therefore, what you might hear for 'I went' is 'Mi es i', but if this follows 'therefore' what you will hear is, 'So mi es i', this instead of the more literary expression, 'Felly euthum'. Another remark might be, 'So ti'n mynd 'te?' (Felly, rwyt ti'n mynd, felly). ''Te', a shortened form of 'ynteu' can also mean 'therefore'.

A person describing a conversation might say, 'So fe ddwedes i' or 'So fe ddwedodd e'. A statement might be expressed thus, 'So fel'na ma(e) hi'. (So that's how it is).

Wales is a Christian country, and we should not jump to conclusions and say that those marauding thieves drank Sir Benjamin's wine. He himself could well have quenched his thirst on his long journey or 'siwrne Dafydd Broffwyd'.

Syr Benjamin Hall a'i gartref, Llanofer

If you ask for any help, beware of fish

Under the influence of superstition, there was once an illogical custom of testing certain women to see if they were witches (gwrachod). The suspect would be tied to a chair at the end of a long see-saw by a deep pool. The chair would be ceremoniously dipped into the pool for long enough for an average person to be in dire danger of drowning. If any woman drowned, it was taken as proof that she was not under the influence of the devil. If any woman survived, it was accepted as proof that she was indeed a witch.

Un cyfieithiad Cymraeg o 'any' yw 'unrhyw' ond byddwch yn ofalus. Mae 'unrhyw' (fel gwrachod) yn gallu bod yn beryglus! Mae rhai pobl yn dweud, 'Nid oedd unrhyw ferched yn y dafarn neithiwr' (There weren't any girls . . .). Mae hyn yn anghywir. Dywedwch, 'Nid oedd merched yn y dafarn neithiwr', neu 'Doedd dim bechgyn yn y capel y bore 'ma'. Falle y byddwch chi'n dweud rhyw ddiwrnod, 'Ni ches i unrhyw anhawster dysgu Cymraeg'. Pan fyddwch chi'n dweud hynny, dydych chi ddim yn siarad Cymraeg cywir. Y frawddeg gywir yw, 'Ni ches i ddim anhawster dysgu Cymraeg'. Ond mae pobl yn gadael y 'ni' allan ac yn dweud, 'Ches i ddim anhawster . . .' Sylwch, dydw i ddim wedi ysgrifennu 'i ddysgu Cymraeg', ond 'dysgu Cymraeg'. Does dim angen yr 'i'.

Ond mae'n gywir dweud (nid, 'Mae'n gywir i ddweud . . .') 'Gwrach yw unrhyw fenyw nad yw'n boddi', neu 'Mae unrhyw fenyw nad yw'n boddi'n wrach'. Cofiwch, does neb byth yn dweud 'unryw' —'unrhyw' yw'r gair bob amser.

Dydy gwrachod ddim yn medru nofio bob amser, ond mae 'gwrachen' yn medru gwneud hynny. Y gair Cymraeg am 'roach' yw 'gwrachen'. Cofiwch, os oes dau wrachen mewn pwll, mae gwrachod yno—hynny yw, pysgod, nid gwragedd!

What I really mean is not what I mean

Just above Llandrindod, not far from the town centre, there is a roadside lake. During the spring spawning season, you might well see a sign warning car drivers: BEWARE OF FROGS. Hundreds of frogs cross the road in order to mate and spawn in the water. In their eagerness to cross, and being oblivious of all highway codes, many are squashed under car wheels. The sign is an attempt to save as many frogs as possible.

Learners should also beware of frogs, mainly because of their relatives, the toads. Maen nhw'n wahanol i'w gilydd. Mae croen broga fel rheol yn llyfn (smooth) ond mae croen llyffant fel rheol yn arw (rough). Mae croen broga'n aml yn wyrdd-felyn, ond mae croen llyffant yn llwyd. Ond dyma'r broblem: Mewn sawl rhan o Gymru, gan amlaf (usually) yn y de, yr enw ar froga yw 'broga' ond mewn rhannau eraill (other parts) o Gymru, gan amlaf yn y gogledd, yr enw ar froga yw 'llyffant'. Maen nhw'n galw'r 'frog' yn 'llyffant cyffredin' ac maen nhw'n galw 'toad' yn 'llyffant dafadennog'.

Nawr, mae Llandrindod yng nghanolbarth Cymru (mid Wales). Yno felly, mae'n anodd gwybod sut mae cael arwydd dwyieithog i helpu'r creaduriaid: GOCHELWCH RHAG Y BROGAOD/LLYFFANTOD CYFFREDIN!

There is another word in Welsh which is growing two directly opposite meanings: it is 'nepell', and is often heard on the news. If someone says, 'Mae'r llyn nepell o Landrindod', you have two choices. To a few it can mean 'far' and to others 'not far', but the most commonly used meaning is the former, so if you wish to say that you live in a village near a particular town, say, 'Rwy'n byw mewn pentre nid nepell o Aberystwyth/Landrindod/Fangor'. A road-crossing frog could say, 'Mae'r llyn nid nepell o'r ffordd', and change its mind upon seeing an approaching car!

Mae'n bwysig gyrru car yn Gymraeg

Mae pobl yn dweud mai'r Rolls Royce yw car gorau'r byd. Arglwydd Llangattock (ger Trefynwy) oedd tad Charles Stewart Rolls. Fe welwch gofgolofn i Charles o flaen neuadd yng nghanol Trefynwy. Mae'r gofgolofn hon yn ein hatgoffa ni (remind us) am gysylltiad (connection) Charles Rolls â Chymru. Dywedodd rhywun wrtho un diwrnod, 'Mae injan car Rolls Royce mor dawel, fe fedrwch chi glywed y cloc yn tician'.

Mae sawl gair Cymraeg pwysig i'r rhai sy'n gyrru (nid 'dreifio') ceir. Fe allwch chi gadw'r car mewn modurdy, ond dydy pobl ddim yn hoffi'r gair hwn. Maen nhw'n dweud 'garej' yn ei le. Cofiwch, mae 'j' yn yr wyddor (alphabet) Gymraeg erbyn hyn. Cyn cychwyn, rhaid cael croniadur/batri (battery) da, un wedi ei wefru (charged). Cofiwch beidio â rhoi dim ond dŵr distyll (distilled water) yn y croniadur. I godi sbîd, medrwch wasgu'r sbardun (throttle). Rydych chi'n medru edrych allan drwy'r sgrîn wynt ar y ffordd. Ambell dro byddwch yn dod at groesffordd (crossroads), dro arall byddwch yn dod at gylchfan (roundabout). Hwyrach y byddwch am droi i ffwrdd ar y chwith neu'r dde. Y gair Cymraeg am 'junction' yw 'cyffordd'. Ond cofiwch ddefnyddio'ch dangosydd (indicator) cyn troi, gan ddefnyddio'r olwyn lywio (steering wheel) wrth gwrs. Pan fyddwch yn mynd yn bell, hwyrach y carech chi fynd ar ffordd ddeuol (dual carriageway) neu draffordd (motorway). Os ych chi am weld a oes digon o olew (oil) yn y car, rhaid ichi dynnu'r ffon ddipio o'r injan. Pan fyddwch yn dod at groesfannau (crossings) edrychwch am bobl yn croesi. Cofiwch fod golau coch a golau melyn yn golygu 'stopiwch'. Mae golau gwyrdd yn golygu 'ewch'.

Cofiwch mai injan (engine) sydd gan gar ac nid peiriant (machine). Wrth iddi losgi tanwydd (fuel) mae'r mwg yn mynd allan trwy'r biben wacáu (exhaust pipe).

Ar ôl clywed am yr injan dawel, dywedodd Charles Rolls wrth ei beiriannydd (engineer). 'Mae gen i gwyn (complaint)—mae'r cloc yn cadw gormod o sŵn!'

Funnily, having fun cannot be fun always

In the nineteenth century Wales was famous for many preachers who went into what was described as 'hwyl' (enthusiasm) when they preached. They would often declaim dramatically in a singing voice, a technique much acclaimed by chapel goers steeped in religious fervour. One of these was Edward Matthews of Ewenni in Glamorgan, one of the foremost preachers of his day. He was born in St Athan in the Vale of Glamorgan. Once, when preaching about the risen Lazarus, he declaimed in his peroration, pointing towards the chapel door, 'A! dacw Lasarus yn dod yn fyw o'r bedd!' (A! There is Lazarus, coming alive from the grave!). Every member of the congregation turned to look, convinced that Lazarus had come to Ewenni.

The word 'hwyl' can be used in many contexts, for example, it is used as a greeting. Expect to hear, 'Bore da. Sut hwyl?' when you meet someone. It can be used also in a farewell statement. A person might say, 'Hwyl iti!' as he/she goes, and have the response, 'Hwyl!' If you desire to wish someone the best of luck in exams, you can say, 'Pob hwyl iti gyda'r arholiade'. If he/she returns with a smile on his/her face, you may ask, 'Gest ti hwyl arni?' If things did not go well, you might hear, 'Na, ches i ddim hwyl arni'. If a son/daughter is rather unwell going to school, you might say to a friend, 'Doedd e/hi ddim yn yr hwylie gore heddi', or you could say about someone who is rather grumpy, 'Mae e/hi'n ddrwg 'i hwyl heddi'.

In another field (or sea) entirely, the Welsh word for 'sail' is 'hwyl'. If a sailor says, 'Rhaid ifi godi'r hwyl', you will know that he is about to sail. The same expression might be used in a concert. A good compere will know that his first task with an audience is to 'codi hwyl'.

Hwyl ichi, a phob hwyl!

We need not pull together together

Wales has two farming unions, the Farmers Union of Wales (FUW) and the National Farmers Union (NFU). The former was established in the late 1950s as many farmers felt that the latter was not doing enough to promote the interests of farmers in Wales. Sometimes the two unions work together, sometimes they do not. There have been many attempts to get them to amalgamate, but the former still feels that the latter lacks a Welsh approach to farming problems and they seem to be as far apart as they ever were.

Fe ddaw hyn â ni at y rhagddodiad (prefix) 'cyd-'. Rydych chi'n ei weld yn aml mewn brawddegau, er enghraifft, 'Mae'r FUW a'r NFU yn cydweithio ambell waith ond dydy eu syniadau nhw ddim yn cyd-fynd'.

In the above example, you will see that 'cydweithio' has no hyphen in its written form but that 'cyd-fynd' has one. This is because the accent in the vast majority of Welsh words falls on the penultimate syllable. In 'cyd-fynd' (and 'cyd-weld') the prefix is the penultimate syllable. The Welsh for 'context' is 'cyd-destun', but the hyphen is used here to differentiate between the consonants 'd' and 'dd'.

If the 'cyd-' refers to people in words of more than two syllables, then the hyphen is used, hence we have 'Cyd-bwyllgor Addysg Cymru' for Welsh Joint Education Committee.

Ambell dro mae 'cyd' ar ddiwedd brawddeg a gallwch ddweud, 'Dyw'r ddau undeb ddim yn gweithio ar y cyd', ond dydy hi ddim yn gywir dweud, 'Dydyn nhw ddim yn cydweithio ar y cyd'. Ambell dro mae rhywun yn dweud, 'Maen nhw'n cydweithio gyda'i gilydd', falle am fod yr ymadrodd (phrase) Saesneg yn dweud 'working together'. Ond does dim rhaid dweud 'cydweithio' a 'gyda'i gilydd'.

Of course, many say that two unions are superfluous. Ych chi'n cyd-fynd?

Try saying it on paper sometimes

At one time it was customary to send a greetings telegram to the reception of newlyweds. This custom started on 24 July 1935. A special greetings telegram was devised by Rex Whistler, the artist. It was enclosed in a golden envelope. With the demise of the telegram, the custom ceased. But before the disappearance of the telegram, special occasion, cheaper to send, greetings cards were devised. The first was issued on 14 February 1936 to celebrate St Valentine's day. Fifty thousand lovers took advantage of this initial offer. Work out how much it cost from this rhyme by a young man:

'And now I've asked you to be mine
By gosh, it's cost me eight and nine!'

Yr enw Cymraeg am 'greetings' yw cyfarchion. Mae busnesau'n anfon slipiau cyfarchion i gwsmeriaid yn aml. Mae hyn yn haws nag anfon llythyr. Ar y slip fe welwch y geiriau: Gyda chyfarchion. Cofiwch fod treiglo'n bwysig yma. Mae'n anghywir dweud: Gyda cyfarchion.

Cyfarchion ffurfiol (formal) yw'r rhain. Os ych chi wedi clywed newyddion da, gallwch anfon llythyr ac ysgrifennu: 'Llongyfarchion', neu os ych chi am longyfarch ffrind ar basio arholiad gallwch ddweud, 'Llongyfarchion ar basio dy arholiad'.

Mae 'llon + cyfarchion' yn rhoi 'llongyfarchion' ichi, ond mae'r 'c' yn treiglo ar ôl yr ansoddair (adjective) 'llon'. Dydy pawb ddim yn dweud 'Llongyfarchion', mae rhai'n dweud 'Llongyfarchiadau'. Lluosog (plural) y gair 'cyfarch' yw 'cyfarchion', a lluosog y gair 'cyfarchiad' yw 'cyfarchiadau'. Mae'r ddau air yn golygu'r un peth erbyn hyn.

Rydyn ni'n defnyddio'r berfenw (verb noun) 'cyfarch' hefyd. Pan fo pobl yn cyfarfod maen nhw'n cyfarch ei gilydd trwy ddweud, 'Bore da' ac ati.

Roedd gan bobl fonheddig slawer dydd 'gyfarchfa' neu ystafell gyfarch yn y tŷ (reception room). Dydyn ni ddim yn defnyddio'r gair hwn heddiw. Rydyn ni'n dweud 'croesawfan' neu 'ystafell groeso' yn lle hynny. The fashion of sending a greetings card goes back a long time. The first one was sent in 1829.

195

The tall tale of the fifty foot cross

Plasty yn ymyl Aberystwyth yw Nanteos. Unwaith roedd cwpan pren diddorol yno. Mae traddodiad (tradition) yn dweud i'r cwpan gael ei wneud o bren y groes. Roedd pobl ofergoelus (superstitious), sâl yn yfed o'r cwpan ac yn dweud, 'Gwyrth (miracle)! Mae'r cwpan wedi fy ngwella i'. Fe gafodd pren y groes ei wneud o bren olewydd (olive) ond fe gafodd cwpan Nanteos ei wneud o bren llwyfen (elm). Dydy e ddim yn hen iawn a dydy e ddim yn Nanteos mwyach.

When learners listen to Welsh speakers, they are often confused by exclamations or mere sentence fillers. The Nanteos cup tale harks back to a time when Wales was Roman Catholic, and it was common for people to cross themselves and say, 'Yn enw'r tad a'r mab a'r ysbryd glân (holy ghost)', making the sign of the cross. This has lost its religious significance but is still used in conversation. Listen for, 'Ie'n tad!' as an affirmative reply to a question. The full response would be, 'Ie, yn enw'r Tad, etc . . .' Even a superstitious learner can content himself with 'ie'. Also you may hear, 'Ie, wir Dduw i ti'. Translated literally, this means, 'God's truth to you'. Someone might say, 'Pren y groes yw cwpan Nanteos, wir Dduw (i ti)!'

The English 'therefore' is often translated as 'felly', and comes at the end of the sentence, the two initial letters having been dropped. Listen for, 'Ble ti'n mynd, 'lly?' The ''lly' has no significance.

Finally, 'ynteu' (then/therefore) can be used as a conjunction, but it is also a common sentence filler. Many speakers use the expression repeatedly and unconsciously in their conversation, usually adding a 'fe'. They could say, 'Mae cwpan Nanteos yn enwog, ynte fe'. But it is not a question.

If all the tales about the holy grail were authentic, the cross would have to have been well over 50 feet high. 'Struth!

Plasty Nanteos

Things are not always as bad as they seem

If you ask the people of Lampeter in Ceredigion for an example of a bad man, they might well think of Sir Herbert Lloyd of Peterwell Mansion. He was hated by family and contemporaries, a man prepared to use any means to achieve an end. There are a few who will say that he was not all bad, but that he was a product of his times. Even his death in 1769 is shrouded in mystery. He died of shotgun wounds, and people think that he committed suicide. Others think that he shot himself accidentally. We shall never know which assumption is correct.

Similarly the Welsh adjective for 'bad'—'drwg', is not all bad. I referred to it on page 144, concentrating on the equative form, 'cynddrwg'. It is sometimes used to prefix composite words. If there is ill feeling between people, we might say, 'Mae drwgdeimlad rhyngddyn nhw'. If you suspect someone of stealing something, you might suggest, 'Rwy'n 'i drwgdybio hi'. If you dislike someone, you could well say, 'Rwy'n 'i drwgleicio hi'.

'Drwg' is used in other ways. Many suffer from wind chaps, and are annoyed if they break out before a party. People sometimes refer to them ruefully as 'cusanau drwg' (bad kisses). If people suspect a misdemeanour, they might say, 'Mae rhyw ddrwg yn y caws', but don't look for cheese. If a man is evil, we say, 'Mae'r dyn yn ddrwg'. But we might also say, 'Mae'r afal yn ddrwg', when an apple is rotten. If we know that someone has received bad tidings we might say, 'Mae hi wedi cael newyddion drwg'.

When talking about children, if they are really wicked, we might say, 'Maen nhw'n blant drwg', but if they are just mischievous, we say, 'Maen nhw'n blant drygionus'. But beware here. If you are teasing someone, she might respond by saying, 'Rych chi'n ddyn drwg/ddynes ddrwg', merely implying that you are naughty. The word must be taken in its context, and if she has a twinkle in her eye, be content.

You might well have to have help with have

You will find the word 'gan' recurring in various forms in the following piece of writing:

Mae gan Ysbyty H M Stanley, Llanelwy, ychydig dros gan gwely ac mae gan Ysbyty Felindre, Caerdydd, ychydig dan gan gwely. Es i Ysbyty Felindre ddoe gan obeithio gweld ffrind, ond gan ei fod wedi mynd adre, welais i mohono fe. Fe brynais i flodau gan siopwr yn y dre cyn mynd yno. Doedd dim newid gen i ac fe roddais i bum can ceiniog (papur pum punt) iddo fe, ond gan fod fy ffrind wedi mynd adre, fe roddais i nhw i rywun arall. Doedd dim blodau gan hwnnw.

I refer again to 'gan' on page 201. It can be quite confusing at times as it can appear in a mutated form, adopt more than one grammatical structure and conjugate.

When you meet someone, you might say, 'Mae'n dda gen (gan) i gwrdd â chi'. He could reply in the same vein and say, 'Mae'n dda gan Huw eich gweld chi hefyd'. But were you to adopt the full form, you would have said, 'Mae'n dda gen(nyf) i gwrdd â chi'.

I have noted previously that more often than not, 'gyda' can be substituted for 'gan' and that learners are often encouraged to concentrate on 'gyda' as they can then ignore the conjugations, but Welsh speakers do conjugate and you must always be aware of what they are saying. There comes a time when you must learn the conjugated forms as they are important; then you should usually be able to follow sentences such as, 'Mae gennym/n ni athro da, ond mae athro gwael ganddyn nhw. Oes athro da gennych chi?' Unfortunately, many of the colloquial forms that you might hear are incorrect, and they are gaining in popularity. Listen for 'Mae ganddon ni (gennym ni) ddigon o amser', or 'Oes ganddoch (gennych) chi amser nawr?' or, 'Does dim arian gin (gen) i', or 'Oes gynnoch (gennych) chi gar newydd?'

Are you saying, 'Let's be having fewer problems, then?'

Do American Indians speak Welsh?

I mentioned on page 29 that Madog ab Owain Gwynedd is reputed to have discovered America long before Columbus did. According to legend, a few of those who landed with him settled in their new country, a few intermarrying with a tribe of Mandan Indians.

To attempt to verify this a young map maker from Caernarfon, John Evans, went to America in 1792 to look for the descendants of these Indians as many were reputed to be blue eyed and able to speak Welsh. He followed the Missouri river for many miles, mapping it as he went along, the first person ever to do so. He was 29 when he died, sad and disillusioned, and was buried in New Orleans.

The Welsh word for 'perhaps' is 'efallai' and is very popular, but it can be as illusive as those Indians and adopts different forms. You will often see the literary form in print but it has been eroded in conversation and you will hardly ever hear 'efallai'. In south Wales, you might hear, 'Falle i Madog lanio yn America', but in north Wales you would hear, 'Ella i John Evans weld yr Indiaid'. 'Falle' and 'Ella' carry the same meaning.

We use still another word which is just as popular—'hwyrach'. You might wish to say, 'Hwyrach i'r Mandaniaid ddysgu Cymraeg', and you may still hear this word in conversation, but you might also hear, 'Wrach mai stori 'di'r cyfan', the emphasis being on the 'w'.

But be wary of 'hwyrach'. It is possible that you might hear, 'Hwyrach fod y bws yn hwyrach nag arfer' (Perhaps the bus is later than usual), as 'hwyrach' can also be the comparative form of the adjective 'hwyr' meaning late.

Perhaps John Evans was too late when he set forth to find the Mandans. Their tribe had become extinct by the nineteenth century. But America is a vast country and they could well be lurking in the vastness somewhere.

Lexicographers work exceedingly slowly and carefully

Mae sawl geiriadur yng Nghymru, ond y geiriadur mwyaf yw *Geiriadur Prifysgol Cymru.* Mae'n cael ei gyhoeddi mewn rhannau (parts). Ymddangosodd y rhan gyntaf yn 1950, pedwar deg chwech o flynyddoedd yn ôl. Ymddangosodd Rhan 44 yn 1995. Does neb yn siŵr pryd y bydd y rhan olaf yn ymddangos (to appear). Mae tîm o bobl yn gweithio ar y geiriadur yma. Maen nhw'n gweithio mewn adeilad ger y Llyfrgell Genedlaethol yn Aberystwyth.

Rydw i wedi sôn am 'gan' ar dudalen 199. Mae 'gan' yn y geiriadur hwn ar dudalen 1379. Mae tudalen gyfan yn egluro (to explain) 'gan'. Mae'n air pwysig iawn.

It often appears in idioms, for example, you can hear, 'Gan amla(f), (usually) mae'n cyrraedd yn gynnar'. If a child is running rather quickly and you wish him (or her) to slow down, you may shout a warning, 'Gan bwyll' which means 'carefully'. You can extend this if you are undertaking a meticulous task and say, 'Gan bwyll bach'. Here, the phrase means 'gently'. In class, you might hear, 'Mae cwningod yn bla. Gan hynny, rhaid lladd cwningod'. Here, 'gan hynny' means 'therefore'.

We have to look upon personal endings here. In grammar books you will read,

Mae gen i	Mae gennym ni
Mae gennyt ti	Mae gennych chi
Mae ganddo ef/hi	Mae ganddyn nhw

This is straightforward, but I noted on page 199 that these personal endings are often 'adjusted' in conversations. Instead of 'Mae gennym/n ni ddigon o amser', you may hear the incorrect form, 'Does ganddon ni ddim arian', 'Mae gynno fo gariad newydd', or even 'Does gento ni ddim . . ./Does gento nhw ddim . . .'

Finally, to confuse you still more, remember that 'gan' comes from an older form, 'can'. It therefore mutates after a conjunction. Listen for, 'Daeth Huw i'r dosbarth a chanddo (nid 'a ganddo') gar newydd, or 'Daeth Gwen i'r tŷ a chanddi gariad newydd', i.e. c > ch. Cofiwch, gan bwyll y mae defnyddio 'gan'.

Think of the position and the situation

St David's Cathedral in St David's and Llandaff Cathedral in Cardiff are two fine cathedrals, but you have to be near to them before you can see them from the west. Both are built in positions that do not meet the eye at once. These positions were chosen carefully, in hollows in the land. At this time, Vikings often invaded Wales in search of treasure, and they were aware that churches were treasure houses. It was safer to hide them as far as possible from the sea. If they could not see a church the avaricious marauders were less likely to land to look for treasure.

Words that have very similar meanings can be a problem for the learner. The word 'safle' (position) is a good example. Do not confuse it with 'sefyllfa' which can mean 'situation, state, condition, etc'. Writing about cathedrals you could say, 'Mae Tyddewi mewn safle (position) da ond beth yw sefyllfa (state) ariannol yr adeilad, tybed? Ydy'r sefyllfa (state) ariannol yn iach ar hyn o bryd, neu ydy'r lle'n debygol o gau?' To make things more awkward, dictionaries offer 'safle' and 'sefyllfa' as the Welsh for 'position', but many would argue that their meanings are subtly different. 'Mae Tyddewi a Llandaf mewn safle da', is preferable to 'Mae Tyddewi a Llandaf mewn sefyllfa dda', if you are talking about where they are situated.

I have previously mentioned 'tebygrwydd' (likeness) and 'tebygolrwydd' (likelihood). If you are avid lottery players, and have read the directions in Welsh, you will note that the writer uses 'tebygrwydd' (likeness), where many would prefer 'tebygolrwydd'.

This brings us to 'money' (arian). 'Sefyllfa ariannol' means 'financial situation', but if you love money, you might be described as 'ariangar'. You could say, 'Mae sefylla ariannol y dyn ariangar o Geredigion yn dda, a'r tebygolrwydd yw na fydd yn prynu ticed loteri. Mae ei gartre mewn safle da ar lan y môr'.

Eglwys Gadeiriol Tyddewi

When you are being personal, avoid the English

Nursery rhymes are an important part of our literature and folk lore. One of the most famous refers to a dear lady who kept a sweet shop in Cydweli. She specialised in selling liquorice, offering ten pieces for a half penny, but 'I' always had an extra piece. The rhyme goes:

> Hen fenyw fach Cydweli
> Yn gwerthu losin du.
> Yn gwerthu deg am ddimai
> Ond un ar ddeg i fi.

'Dimai' is almost obsolete as we no longer deal in halfpennies. Note how 'un ar ddeg' is set—as three separate words, with no hyphen. This is true for all numerals. Do not write 'un-deg-chwech', for example.

But the last word of the rhyme has been causing much trouble to learners with their ears tuned to idiomatic expressions. The old lady of Cydweli, referring to her store would say, 'Fy siop i'. She might also say, 'Rwyf fi yn gwerthu losin du yn fy siop i'.

'Fi' in this instance is a dependent pronoun, but it is nearly always decapitated (quite correctly) in conversation. The rule is, 'fi' nearly always becomes 'i' but if the preceding word ends in 'f' you may use 'fi'. The old lady, therefore, could have said 'Rwyf fi', or 'Rwyf i'.

But she would never say, 'Mae siop fi', an alien expression that is creeping more and more into the language under the influence of English (My shop, etc.). A child might say in school, 'Dw i 'di colli llyfr fi'. He/she should be corrected, as the correct expression is, 'Dw i 'di colli fy llyfr i'. Never say, 'Mae dosbarth fi nos Wener', but use the expression, 'Mae (fy) nosbarth i nos Wener', the personal pronoun after the verb 'to be' being dropped.

Should it be possible for that old lady to come back, she should punish those that translate directly from the English by refusing to sell them sweets.

A bit of a coffin in a dresser to remember

Whilst travelling in north-east Wales I stumbled upon an interesting tradition. I was in a house that had a fine dresser and I noted that small rectangular pieces of wood had been bedded in the wood in three different places. I assumed that they had been used to repair knot holes, but the owner explained that at one time, it was traditional to cut a tiny rectangular piece from the coffin (arch) of the departed before a funeral and bed it in the dresser, providing a link between the dead person and his or her home and family.

People nowadays use the English word for 'coffin' but you will also come across the Welsh word, 'arch', though it was at one time used for other chests and coffers. The bible informs us that Noah and his retinue sailed the world in an 'arch' (ark).

The most common word for 'rainbow' is 'enfys' but many refer to it as 'bwa'r arch' (colloquially 'bwa'r a'ch'), a reminder of God's traditional promise not to drown the world again, but the word is also common as a prefix (meaning 'chief') to many words. One of the most important people during National Eisteddfod week is the 'archdderwydd' (archdruid/the chief druid) of the Gorsedd; the Church has its 'archesgob' (archbishop), and even God traditionally has his 'archangel' (archangel).

The word 'arch' also means 'a request' or 'a command', though you will hardly ever hear it used as such in conversation. In the eisteddfod chairing ceremony the archdruid will ask the poet to arise at the call of the trumpet (ar alwad yr utgorn/y corn gwlad). He could say, 'Ar arch y corn gwlad'.

But the letters 'arch' crop up at the beginning of a very commonly used word, 'archeb' (plural 'archebion', verb 'archebu') for 'order'. You might say, 'Rhaid ifi archebu llaeth sgim bob wythnos'. They also emerge at the end of words such as 'cyfarch' (greeting). A compliments slip translates as 'cyfarchlen'.

Remember to call if you're passing the castle

There is no call for castle accommodation in Wales today. Most castles were built by the Normans but a few were built by the Welsh themselves. They built their first earthwork construction at Welshpool (Trallwng) around 1115. In 1171, they began to build their first stone and mortar castle at Cardigan (Castell Aberteifi). They began their last one at Caergwrle (Hope) in 1277.

'There is no call for castles' translates as 'Does dim galw am gestyll'. Here the word 'galw' fulfils one of its many functions. If you wish someone to call to see you, you will say, 'Cofiwch alw nawr/rŵan'. Here it takes the soft mutation, dropping the initial 'g'. If you rephrase the sentence and say, 'Peidwch ag anghofio galw', there is no mutation. 'Thingummybob', is a useful English description of that elusive article that escapes the memory. In Welsh, we say, 'Be ti/chi'n galw'. If you forget that the Welsh for table is 'bwrdd/bord', you can say, 'Rho fe ar y be ti/chi'n galw'.

A child might complain to his mother about name calling in school, 'Mam, ma'n nhw'n galw enwe arna i'. If you wish to say to someone that you intend dropping by later, you might say, 'Fe fydda i'n galw heibio'n nes ymla(e)n'. If a miscreant is called to give an account of his dirty deeds, we say, 'Mae fe 'di cael 'i alw i gyfri(f)'.

To return to that elusive word, you might say, 'Alla/Fedra i ddim cofio'r gair', or you can use 'galw' and say, 'Fedra i ddim galw'r gair i gof'.

The noun is 'galwad' and is also worked hard. If you wish to tell someone that you made an emergency (999) call on the telephone, you say, 'Fe wnes i alwad frys'. Again, note the mutations.

There never has been a call for castles as ideal places of abode, but Chirk Castle has been in continuous occupation since it was built in the thirteenth century. Cofiwch alw heibio rywbryd. Rhowch alwad ffôn cyn dod.

Castell y Waun

Behold the three bodied saint with three graves

Llandaff Cathedral in Cardiff is consecrated to Saint Teilo, who was born in Penalun (Penally in its corrupt Anglicised form) in Pembrokeshire. He established other churches, including Llandeilo, in Carmarthenshire. Traditionally he has been buried in three graves, because we in Wales cannot seem to reach a consensus about anything. Tradition informs us that he died at Llandaff but it was decided to carry his body to his birthplace. He was placed in Llandeilo church on the way and the monks began to bicker regarding where he should be laid to rest, Penalun, Llandaff and Llandeilo arguing their respective corners. When they returned to the church, they found that there were now three bodies, so they took one each. A convenient miracle!

There are many words to describe a burial in Welsh. A very common one is 'angladd', often pronounced 'anglodd'. You can ask, 'Pryd mae'r angladd?' The person in charge of the funeral was once called an 'angladdwr'. Nowadays, a translation of 'undertaker', 'ymgymerwr' is used. At one time it was customary to have a 'pregeth angladdol' (funeral sermon) in the church/chapel of the deceased. This word is not common in north Wales. There, they favour, 'cynhebrwng', which roughly means 'accompanying together'. The word 'hebrwng' is often used by sweethearts, and a suitor may ask a girl, 'Gaf i dy hebrwng di adre heno?' But north Walians use a shortened form for funeral and might say, 'Mae'r cnebrwng fory'. Still another word is 'arwyl'. It is centuries old and is still used though a few confuse it with 'arlwy' (feast). Many use the word 'claddedigaeth', and people might ask, 'Pryd mae'r gladdedigaeth?' or even use the verb form and inquire, 'Pryd maen nhw'n claddu?' Even when the deceased person is being cremated (amlosgi) in a crematorium (amlosgfa) they will still refer to the 'claddedigaeth'. The most common Welsh word for 'cemetery' is 'mynwent', but 'claddfa' (burial place) is used in many parts of Wales; however, one cemetery that we do not wish to see is one for the Welsh language. Years ago many forecast its demise, but it has many helping hands at the moment to assist it to view the future with hope.